Kingfisher

Kingfisher

DAVID CHANDLER AND IAN LLEWELLYN

NH
NEW HOLLAND

Published in 2010 by New Holland Publishers (UK) Ltd
London • Cape Town • Sydney • Auckland
www.newhollandpublishers.com
Garfield House, 86–88 Edgware Road, London W2 2EA, United Kingdom
80 McKenzie Street, Cape Town 8001, South Africa
Unit 1, 66 Gibbes Street, Chatswood, NSW 2067, Australia
218 Lake Road, Northcote, Auckland, New Zealand

10 9 8 7 6 5 4 3 2 1

A catalogue record for this book is available from the British Library

ISBN 978 1 84773 524 9

Publisher: Simon Papps
Publishing Director: Rosemary Wilkinson
Project Editor: Beth Lucas
Design: Roger Hammond at Blue Gum Designers
Cover design: Jason Hopper
Production: Melanie Dowland

Reproduction by PDQ Digital Media Solutions Ltd, UK
Printed and bound in Singapore by Tien Wah Press (Pte) Ltd

All photographs by Ian Llewellyn except for the following:
Niall Benvie/naturepl.com: p23; Angelo Gandolfi/naturepl.com: p92 and p95;
Phil Palmer: p18, p20 and p22; Photolibrary.com: p15, p84, p89 and p90;
Photoshot: pp12-13 and p16; and Wiki Commons: p37.

In memory of Keith Morris, a good man, who was
passionate about certain waterside hunters…

DAVID CHANDLER

For Alyson, Jem, Fen and Rodney, my shining stars.

IAN LLEWELLYN

Contents

Preface

I was fourteen years old when I saw my first Common Kingfisher. It was 3 December 1978 and I was birdwatching with a friend at gravel pits in Berkshire in southern England. My records of the moment simply say that the Kingfisher was 'seen in flight' – it was clearly a very typical encounter with the 'blue blur'.

As a teenage volunteer I worked for the RSPB at Minsmere, a nature reserve on England's east coast. My task one day was the early morning Marsh Harrier watch, which involved sitting in a hide and recording everything the Marsh Harriers did. I still have good memories of prolonged views of a Kingfisher that perched about five metres from me that morning.

Over subsequent decades, Kingfishers have brightened my life on many occasions. Often, they have been just a blur, but sometimes they have been so much more.

Some years later I was privileged to visit the Camargue, a fantastic wetland in the south of France. I saw seven Kingfishers that day: still my record. Today, my local patch is a country park near Cambridge and it is a good place to see Kingfishers. I see them more often than not, perhaps most memorably during an early morning visit when I stumbled upon a Kingfisher perched about 25 metres away. I saw it dive and bring its breakfast back to its perch, where it whacked the fish against a branch to prepare it for swallowing.

This juvenile female Kingfisher is adopting an upright threat posture.

There is something about Kingfishers. No matter how many times you have seen them, they can still make a day special, and prompt excited exclamations. With the blue blur, familiarity doesn't breed contempt. I have enjoyed seeing other members of the kingfisher family in the Americas and Africa, but the Common Kingfisher, the only species that is found regularly in the UK, remains a favourite.

Many people have worked on Kingfishers, but there are two studies that have been particularly helpful in writing this book and that merit specific mention. The first is Ron and Rosemary Eastman's work. The

Eastmans were talented wildlife film-makers, whose film *Private Life of the Kingfisher* was first broadcast in 1966. This award-winning film featured Kingfishers on the River Test, in Hampshire, southern England, and was repeated no less than eight times. Rosemary's book, *The Kingfisher*, was published in 1969. The second is David Boag's study, over seven years, in Dorset, another southern English county, which was first published in 1982. The book you are reading now would have been the poorer without their labours – so thank you Ron, Rosemary and David.

Ian Llewellyn, who took most of the pictures in this book, is a wildlife cameraman and stills photographer – someone who knows what it is like to spend many hours in a hide. Ian has been pointing lenses at Kingfishers for over five years, and has seen some remarkable behaviour, including things that may not have been recorded before, such as parents feeding their young on crayfish. This book adds his observations to the established wisdom to provide a fresh look at the Common Kingfisher. It is not the definitive statement on the bird; it would be impossible to capture every variation of behaviour and call and there are still discoveries to be made. My hope is that the book presents a well-researched biography in a way that is enjoyable and easy to read. Not too heavy, but still comprehensive. It has been written for anyone who wants to know more about Kingfishers, from those with little previous knowledge to more studious and experienced birdwatchers.

Many readers will have seen a Common Kingfisher, perhaps several times. But however long you have been watching this gem of a bird, I suspect that you will find something here that will be new to you. The book starts with a concise overview of the kingfisher family before introducing the Common Kingfisher more fully. Successive chapters then look at specific aspects of the bird's life, and conclude with a look at its changing fortunes and some practical hints about how to see one.

I hope you enjoy the book, and that it encourages you to spend some time with the blue blur. Perhaps your observations will add to our understanding of this much-loved bird.

David Chandler

Opposite: A blue blur is captured streaking into the entrance to its tunnel on a riverbank. Such a low nesting site could be risky for this Kingfisher and its family, increasing the threat from flooding or predation.

1 | The kingfisher family

In most of Europe there is only one kingfisher, *Alcedo atthis*, a blue and orange gem that, because there aren't any others, we simply call the 'Kingfisher', although it is more correctly known as the Common Kingfisher. In most of this book, I have used the term 'Kingfisher' to mean 'Common Kingfisher' as this is what most people say in everyday speech. In this chapter however, 'kingfisher' is used to encompass other kingfisher species too. Its more formal common name and its scientific name distinguish the Common Kingfisher from over 90 other kingfisher species that can be found around the world. Exactly how many other kingfisher species there are is uncertain – bird taxonomy doesn't stay still for long and different authorities have reached different conclusions.

It is not just the number of species that differs. The International Ornithological Congress (IOC) puts the kingfishers in one family, the Alcedinidae, alongside five other families in the order Coraciiformes: the rollers (Coraciidae); the ground rollers (Brachypteraciidae) of Madagascar; the todies (Todidae), found only in the Caribbean; the motmots (Momotidae) of the neotropics; and the 'sting-defying' bee-eaters (Meropidae). The kingfishers total more species than all of the other families put together (58 species). An alternative classification treats the Alcedinidae as not one family, but three: the river kingfishers (Alcedinidae), the tree kingfishers (Halcyonidae) and the water kingfishers (Cerylidae). The species' names and taxonomy that I have used in this chapter follow the IOC classification.

Structure and colour

The kingfisher 'design template' includes a big head on a chunky, short-necked body, short legs, a stumpy tail and a long, dagger-like bill. They have very good vision whether above or below the water surface, thanks, in part at least, to elliptical lenses. At just 10cm (4in) from bill-tip to tail-tip, and tipping the scales at a mere 10g (0.4oz) or so, the aptly named African Dwarf Kingfisher (*Ispidina lecontei*) really is the dwarf of the family, not to be confused with the similarly named, but larger, African Pygmy Kingfisher (*Ispidina picta*), which is two centimetres longer. The Giant Kingfisher (*Megaceryle maxima*) is at the other end of

Previous page: The vibrant Rufous-backed Kingfisher (*Ceyx rufidorsa*) is found across a very large range in Thailand, Malaysia, Indonesia and the Philippines.

the scale. Found in much of sub-Saharan Africa, at 45cm (18in) long and with a mean weight of 355g (13oz), this is Africa's heavyweight. But the real giants among kingfishers are in Australasia. The Laughing Kookaburra is a similar length to the Giant Kingfisher, but can reach 500g (18oz).

The kingfisher's bill is one of its most striking features. As a vital feeding tool, its structure indicates something of the owner's diet. A bird that eats mostly fish, for example Australasia's Little Kingfisher (*Ceyx pusilla*), has a pointed bill that looks like it has been squeezed at the sides, while one that prefers to dine on insects and other invertebrates, such as Africa's Striped Kingfisher (*Halcyon chelicuti*), which feeds mainly on grasshoppers, has a shorter, flatter bill. No other kingfisher has a bill like that of the Shovel-billed Kookaburra (*Clytoceyx rex*). This unusual bird, found only in New Guinea, sits in a genus all of its own. It is big, measuring 33cm (13in) in length, and sports a stout, squat, cone-shaped bill that is clearly not the bill of a fish-eater. In fact, it forages in damp soil and mud for earthworms, insects, snails and lizards.

At the other end of the body, kingfishers have weak feet with three or four toes. A four-toed kingfisher has three toes pointing forwards and one pointing backwards, an arrangement common to most birds. Three-toed species lack the innermost forward-facing toe. All kingfishers have feet that are syndactyl; on each foot, two of the toes are joined for some of their length. The middle and outer toes are joined for more than half their length, and, if an inner toe is present, about a third of that is fused to the middle toe too.

The family has been lavishly adorned from the colour palette, and many species are a combination of blue and orange. References to blue are

The Sacred Kingfisher, (*Todiramphus sanctus*) is found in Australasia, Fiji and Indonesia. It is not as spectacularly coloured as some other members of the family but has the characteristic body shape and a powerful bill. The diet of this species includes a variety of small vertebrates and arthropods, including crabs.

Some surprises

The kingfisher family as a whole may not be quite as you imagine it…

- Not all kingfisher species live by rivers and lakes. Some live a long way from water, and more than half of them live in forested areas.

- Not all members of the family have 'kingfisher' in their name, though the vast majority do. The exceptions are the five species of Australasian kookaburras.

- For some species, 'fisher' is a misnomer. None of them survive on fish alone, and some species, such as the Shovel-billed Kookaburra (*Clytoceyx rex*), get most of their sustenance from terrestrial invertebrates.

- Not all kingfishers are diurnal (active during daylight hours). New Guinea's Hook-billed Kingfisher (*Melidora macrorrhina*) is active at dawn and dusk and perhaps at night.

- Bird ringers have discovered that when a Common Kingfisher is being held in the hand, if it is laid on its back it will make no attempt to fly off.

Australia's Laughing Kookaburra, seen here with an unfortunate legless lizard, is one of the few family members that does not take the name 'kingfisher'.

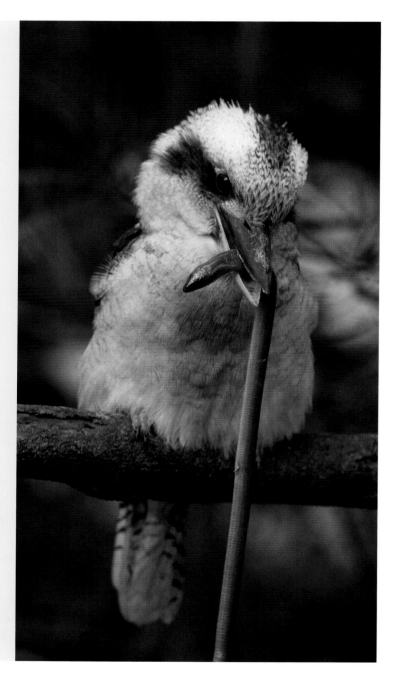

a recurrent theme in their common names: Cobalt Paradise Kingfisher (*Tanysiptera carolinae*), Lazuli Kingfisher (*Todiramphus lazuli*), Ultramarine Kingfisher (*Todiramphus leucopygius*), Azure Kingfisher (*Ceyx azurea*), Malachite Kingfisher (*Alcedo cristata*) and Cerulean Kingfisher (*Alcedo coerulescens*), and numerous mentions of plain old blue, including blue-winged, blue-breasted, blue-banded, shining-blue and blue-eared. The blue-and-orange theme can be seen on kingfishers in many parts of the world, including Asia, Africa and Australia, but those in the *Ceryle, Chloroceryle* and *Megaceryle* genera are painted from a different palette. North America's Belted Kingfisher (*Megaceryle alcyon*) and the Pied Kingfisher (*Ceryle rudis*) of Africa and Asia are good examples. The males and females of most kingfisher species look similar, and juveniles are a toned down version of the adults. Paradise kingfishers are an exception – the drab juveniles look quite different to the adult birds.

Where do they live?
Kingfishers are found on every continent apart from Antarctica, and are also absent from far northern latitudes. To see the greatest diversity of kingfishers, head to Australasia or the tropics of Africa and Asia. Cameroon is home to 12 species from five different genera. Borneo, Sumatra, Java and Bali host 14 species in seven genera and Australia has 11 species in five different genera. There are even kingfishers on some very remote Pacific islands, including the Mewing Kingfisher (*Todiramphus ruficollaris*) of the Cook Islands and the Chattering Kingfisher (*T. tutus*) on the Society Islands. In terms of kingfisher diversity, Europe is definitely impoverished. If you include the three records of Belted Kingfisher between 1950 and 2007, the British kingfisher lists peaks at just two species from two genera, and it is only the Common Kingfisher that occurs regularly. Two more species can be added for Europe as a whole, with small populations of White-throated Kingfisher (*Halcyon smyrnensis*) resident in Turkey and Azerbaijan, and populations of Pied Kingfisher (*Ceryle rudis*) living in Turkey and Cyprus.

Kingfishers are not found in every habitat in the countries in which they occur, but they do occur in a wide range of habitats. Many people think of kingfishers as birds of lakes and rivers, and while this is accurate for some species, for many it is not. Kingfishers live on coral atolls, up mountains, in mangroves, deep in rainforests, on seashores and in savannahs. Perhaps surprisingly, more species live in forests, with or without streams, than in other habitats. Less surprisingly, most deserts are kingfisher-free zones, but even this is not a universal truth – in Australia, the Red-backed Kingfisher (*Todiramphus pyrrhopygius*) survives in seriously arid desert.

Opposite: The African Dwarf Kingfisher is the smallest member of the family. This tiny bird lives in dark rainforest habitats, where it feeds on small insects.

What do they eat?

Contrary to what you might think, most species don't depend on fish. Some do take fish, but the family's diet sheet lists a host of invertebrates including crabs, earthworms, molluscs, centipedes, spiders, various insects and an impressive range of non-fish vertebrates too, including small mammals, tadpoles, frogs, birds, snakes and other reptiles. The Belted Kingfisher (*Megaceryle alcyon*) even feeds on plant material occasionally. Generally speaking, waterside kingfishers are primarily fish-eaters, and species that live in dry places eat other things. Some species are picky eaters, with a limited range of prey items making up most of their diet. The Pied Kingfisher (*Ceryle rudis*), which is primarily a bird of Africa, Asia and the Middle East, and the Green Kingfisher (*Chloroceryle americana*) of the Americas are examples of species that eat mainly fish. Others are much less discerning. The Sacred Kingfisher (*Todiramphus sanctus*) for example, which is found in Australasia and Indonesia and on various Pacific Islands, will eat a host of invertebrates, as well as reptiles, amphibians, birds, mammals and fish. Even the specialist fishers, such as the Common Kingfisher, supplement their fishy meals with invertebrates.

The Common Kingfisher's familiar perch–watch–dive–perch approach to hunting is not the only technique the kingfisher family uses to find the next meal. The family's food-gathering skills include diving from a hover, which gives a Pied Kingfisher access to prey up to two metres (6.5ft) beneath the water's surface. This species, and the Belted Kingfisher, hover

Pied Kingfisher *Ceryle rudis*

Pied Kingfishers are found in Africa and Asia, including the Middle East, with smaller numbers in south-east Europe. The species is unique among kingfishers in being a colonial nester. Normally, this occurs when suitable nesting habitat is hard to come by and not alongside the feeding area. Some are solitary breeders, however, and will stake their claim to a length of river where they build their nest and fish.

Parents benefit from the contributions of primary and/or secondary 'helpers'.

Typically, a primary helper is a one-year-old male offspring of one or more of the parents. Secondary helpers are thought to be unrelated birds that are either not breeding or that tried to breed earlier that year but failed.

Helpers assist with feeding the breeding birds and their young, and provide extra muscle to drive off interlopers or predators. A pair may benefit from the contributions of several secondary helpers but normally has just one primary helper.

up to 12 metres (39ft) above the surface of the water. Hovering is not widespread among kingfishers, however – only seven species can do it and these are the most fish-dependent species, including the Common Kingfisher. Despite the family name, many species, including those in the *Tanysiptera* and *Halcyon* genera, and the *Dacelo* kookaburras, feed terrestrially, though they may take food from the water surface too. Their technique is a bit like the aquatic fishers, but with a swoop rather than a dive, and prey is picked off the ground or plants, including trees. Some species – Africa's *Halcyon* kingfishers, for example – snatch insects in flight. Australia's Red-backed Kingfishers have even been caught in the act of breaking into the mud nests of Fairy Martins (*Petrochelidon ariel*) to steal some young avian protein. Laughing Kookaburras (*Dacelo novaeguineae*) can be thieves too, using surprise as a tactic to grab food from the hands of picnicking humans. They will take snakes too.

Some food items receive special treatment before swallowing. Among fish-eaters, the coup de grâce may be administered by bashing the victim against a perch, and this can break bones and make sharp spines safer to swallow. Similar behaviour is also exhibited by other kingfishers, with terrestrial prey being bashed against a perch or on the ground.

The Common Kingfisher doesn't just feast on fish. This individual has caught a damselfly larva.

The mating game

Typically, kingfishers are monogamous. Most can probably breed when they are one year old and will seek to evict others of their species from their territory, sometimes with considerable determination. Elaborate courtship displays do not seem to be common in kingfishers, though those in the *Halcyon* genus will belt out a song from the top of a tree, twisting from side to side with wings held open.

Kingfishers nest in holes – in trees, termite nests and earth banks. Tree-nesters include Australia's Laughing Kookaburra and Africa's Woodland Kingfisher (*Halcyon senegalensis*), which will move into a woodpecker or barbet hole. Many forest-dwelling kingfishers will use termite nests (termitaria), as their nest sites, digging into the insects' handiwork at ground level or, as in the Micronesian Kingfisher (*Todiramphus cinnamominus*) on the island of Pohnpei for example, up in the treetops. The earth bank nesters, including the Common Kingfisher, excavate a tunnel in waterside banks, including man-made banks. With a tunnel of eight-and-a-half metres long (over 27ft) the Giant Kingfisher holds the record for the longest nest tunnel of any kingfisher. Creating a nest site can be dangerous for a kingfisher. Sometimes, as work commences, a bird will launch itself at what it hopes will become the nest entrance with such zeal that he or she is mortally wounded.

Opposite: White-breasted Kingfisher (*Halycon smyrnensis*) is found in many habitats from Turkey to the Philippines.

Whatever the nest site, kingfishers lay shiny, white eggs that are incubated by both parents, though scientists think that, generally, the female does the bulk of the work. Within the family, clutch sizes range from one to ten eggs. Species of temperate latitudes have bigger clutches, averaging roughly 6–7 eggs, than those of tropical regions, which average 3–4 eggs. Typically, the eggs don't all hatch at the same time – those that were laid first hatch first. This means that when the male and female bring food to their young, they will be feeding chicks of different sizes and different ages. The clutch of 4–8 Common Kingfisher eggs, however, hatches more or less synchronously.

The distinctive Giant Kingfisher (above) typically excavates a tunnel two metres long. This species is responsible for the longest kingfisher tunnel on record, at 8.5 metres.

The challenges of raising young are made easier for Pied Kingfishers and Laughing Kookaburras by assistance from 'helpers' – individuals of the same species that help the parent birds (see also page 20).

2 | Introducing the Common Kingfisher

For Europeans on their home ground, Kingfisher identification is simple. It is not always easy to see a Kingfisher, but when you do, you are likely to recognize it. In almost the whole of Europe (excepting Turkey, Cyprus and Azerbaijan), there is only one kingfisher species – the Common Kingfisher (*Alcedo atthis*). *Alcedo* simply means kingfisher, and this species is named after *Atthis*, a particularly attractive lady who lived on the Mediterranean island of Lesbos around 600BC. There are 11 other species in the *Alcedo* genus and of all the kingfisher genera, only *Todiramphus* has more species, with 22 representatives.

It would be hard to confuse the Kingfisher with anything else and many people who have never seen one know what it looks like. They may not know how to tell a male from a female, or a juvenile from an adult, but even that is pretty straightforward given a half-decent view.

Small and colourful

The Kingfisher is definitely not an LBJ (or Little Brown Job, as many birders describe small drab birds that they can't easily identify). It *is* little though. Measured from bill-tip to tail-tip, a Kingfisher is just 16–17cm (6.5in) long, and roughly a quarter of this length is made up of its bill. It has short, rounded wings that span 24–26cm (9.4–10.2in) when spread. An adult weighs between 34g and 46g (1.2–1.6oz). To put this in perspective, you could post two big ones, or very nearly three small ones, for the price of a standard letter, assuming you could get them into the envelope.

To describe this bird as blue and orange doesn't do justice to its stunning plumage, especially the range of blues, which in some lights can look green. Capturing these wonderful colours in words is not easy – it is hard to define the exact blue of a Kingfisher, not least because it isn't just one colour. The most striking blue is on the tail and back, and this can be seen particularly well on a bird in flight. It is just the tips of the feathers that produce this blast of colour, but because of the way the feathers overlap it is only the tips that we see. This blue is described as 'electric' and 'shifting from azure to cobalt'.

Previous page: An alert male. The distinctive Kingfisher is easy to recognize, but not so easy to see.

Opposite: It is no wonder that this beautiful bird is so popular. The lovely plumage, seen here on a female, is most striking on the tail and back.

Below: Feathers from a juvenile Kingfisher's back and breast.

The colour changes that we see are caused by the structure of the feathers rather than being solely about pigments. Their structure is such that when light hits them the blue wavelengths are scattered more than the red ones, a phenomenon known as the Tyndall effect. Where there is 'electricity' in the Kingfisher's plumage the blues are not static, and these areas can take on different tones in different light conditions, adding yet more sparkle. To be strictly accurate, the electric blue 'tail' is not actually the tail, but the upper-tail coverts. These are smaller feathers that cover the base of the tail, and in the Kingfisher's case, much of the rest of the tail too. The true tail lies underneath and is a darker blue.

Elsewhere on the bird, there is less 'voltage'. The blue on the wings and head is darker, and can appear greener in some light conditions. The

Kingfisher back and tail feathers under the microscope. The shimmering electric blue is due to the structure of the feathers, not just the pigmentation.

Male and female
Kingfishers are similar in
appearance, but with
careful observation they
can be told apart. The
male (above) has a
completely black bill, but
the lower mandible of the
female (below) has
reddish or orange on it.

forehead, crown, nape, and the bar that descends from the base of the bill are brighter and some of the wing coverts (small feathers that cover the bases of the flight feathers) are also tipped with a bolt of blue.

For one so bright, the Kingfisher can be easy to overlook, and you may not notice it until your presence disturbs it and forces it to fly – low, fast and with whirring wings. Somehow those tropical colours don't always betray the bird's presence, and a perched bird can be surprisingly hard to spot among waterside vegetation.

Male or female?

If you can see an adult bird well enough, male and female can be told apart, but not by their plumage. The clue is in the bill. If is the bird is male, the bill is black. If it is female the lower mandible is mostly reddish or orange, perhaps with a hint of brown, with the black restricted to the tip. The size of the black tip varies, but it is usual for it to cover one sixth to one quarter of the length of the bill, although it can be as much as two thirds, and on a few individuals the black is completely absent. Some males do have a bit of colour at the base of their lower mandible – ill-defined muted red or orangey blobs, or a suggestion of brown perhaps.

Juveniles look like muted adults. The tip of the bill is pale in both males and females for many months after fledging. This fledgling has been out of the nest for just three days.

Adult or juvenile?

Juveniles look like muted adults, with more green, less blue, and blue-grey tones on the breast. When they fledge, both males and females have an off-white tip to an otherwise black bill. The pale tip remains for many months, and might still be visible the following spring, but not all of the black remains. Young birds leave the nest from the second half of May to the beginning of October, and about four weeks later, pinkish blobs appear at the base of the lower mandible. In the female, these get bigger and bigger and by January a chick's gender may be obvious, though it may take 8–12 months before the bill looks more or less adult. Working out the gender of a juvenile can be tricky while the lower mandible colour is developing, but the pinkish blobs on a male cover no more than a third of the bill.

A fresh-out-of-the-nest juvenile has black legs and feet. Those of the adults are almost fluorescent orange, and the slow, progressive brightening of a youngster's legs provides clues to its age. Normally, the legs stay black for around 8–11 weeks. Then the red pigment surfaces, taking four to five months to transform black legs to glorious ruddy appendages.

The Kingfisher's new coat

Feather care is a vital aspect of any bird's life and every Kingfisher will devote a significant amount of time to keeping its plumage in good shape. But the feathers of even the most fastidious bird will need to be replaced from time to time.

The first moult takes juveniles to their first adult plumage. Kingfishers leave the nest during a period that can span more than four months of the year. As a consequence, some juveniles start moulting in July, but some have not started by December. This is not a complete moult – it involves at least some of the feathers on the head and body and perhaps some tail feathers (more on some birds than others), but not the flight feathers. When winter closes in, moulting stops whether the moult has been completed or not. If necessary the moult begins again in the spring. At this point some brand new inner flight feathers may appear too.

Adults moult after breeding, from June onwards. This moult involves most or all of their feathers, including the flight feathers, though the body feathers are the first to be renewed. Primary feathers are not shed until the new ones are well grown. By the end of November, if not before, the moult may be completed, though as in the post-juvenile moult, it may grind to a halt as winter approaches, and be continued in

Opposite: This young female is moulting for the first time. When the moult is complete she will have adult plumage.

the next year. It is not unusual for the moult of one wing to be out of synch with the other. The tail moult may be 'unbalanced' too, and it seems that the older the bird gets, the more asymmetric its moult becomes. Unless it is really cold, body feathers may be lost and renewed at almost any time, and some plumage may be moulted twice a year.

How common is the Common Kingfisher?

BirdLife International estimates the world population of Common Kingfishers at 600,000 birds and the European population at up to 160,000 pairs. The species lives in lots of different countries and, globally speaking, conservation scientists see little cause for concern.

At a European level, however, things are not quite as rosy, but there is no major cause for concern. BirdLife International regard this species as of 'European Conservation Concern'. They classify it as 'SPEC 3' – a 'Species of European Conservation Concern, category 3'. Apart from 'Non-SPEC' species, which are not of conservation concern, this is the least worrying category – birds that are believed to be at greater risk are 'SPEC 1 or 2'. The Kingfisher has this label because its population suffered 'moderate decline' from 1970 to 1990, and there are still fewer of them than there were before 1970.

Closer to home, *Birds of Conservation Concern 3*, published by a

Kingfishers may devote up to two hours a day to preening their feathers, using the bill to apply oil from the preen gland. Diligent care of feathers is vital for birds that are frequently immersed in water when they dive for food.

consortium of conservation organisations in 2009, summarizes the population status of the UK's bird species and places the Kingfisher on its amber list, signifying that the species is of moderate conservation concern. The red list is the birds that are most urgently in need of help.

The UK breeding population is estimated at 4,800–8,000 pairs. For comparison, the UK is also home to about 150 pairs of Ospreys (*Pandion haliaetus*), and about 8.5 million Winter Wren *Troglodytes troglodytes* territories. (The wren's population is expressed as territories because one male wren may breed with more than one female in his territory.)

Different looks and different places

The Kingfisher is not just a bird of Europe. Its range extends from Ireland, Portugal and Morocco in the west, eastwards through continental Europe and discontinuously across Asia as far as Japan and Sakhalin. Birds in southern Sweden, Finland and adjacent parts of Russia are the northernmost breeders. Further south, you can find Common Kingfishers in India and China and down into Thailand and Malaysia. Keep going south and you can still see the same kingfisher species as you see in Europe – they are found in Indonesia, the Philippines and Papua New Guinea. You can even find them in the Solomon Islands. But you won't find any in the Americas, Australia, or sub-Saharan Africa – you will have to content yourself with other kingfisher species in these areas.

The Kingfisher comes in more than one form. The Clements checklist of December 2008 (one of about four published lists of the world's bird species) names seven different subspecies, each denoted by a different suffix to the two-part specific name (the IOC list does not include subspecies). In Europe there are two subspecies, *Alcedo atthis atthis* (the 'nominate' form), and *A. a. ispida*. *Alcedo atthis atthis* is found around the Mediterranean, in south-east Europe and in European Russia. Kingfishers seen further north and west are of the subspecies *ispida*. The average birdwatcher, or even the above average birdwatcher, might wonder what all the fuss is about. There are minor differences in colour and size, but the difference can be as small as half a millimetre of wing-length, and even the best binoculars in the world will not spot that. To make it even harder, that wing-length difference is not totally reliable.

Brief encounters

Many people's experience of the Kingfisher is a snatched glimpse of turquoise flying away and out of sight. They can fly fairly fast – estimates suggest speeds of at least 40–45 kilometres per hour (25–28 miles per hour) on a still day. To pick them up more efficiently, try to learn their call, a piercing and high-pitched whistle. If you hear it, scan low over the water for a bird in flight.

A fleeting glimpse is all many people see of a Kingfisher. They can reach speeds of up to 45 km per hour or more.

Myth and Legend

A French legend tells a story of how the Kingfisher acquired its wonderful colours. The legend says that on Noah's ark, the Kingfisher was a grey bird, and when Noah got fed up waiting for the dove to come back after it had been sent out to find somewhere dry he enlisted the services of the Kingfisher. But, to escape a storm, the Kingfisher flew very high and got struck by lightning, which gave the bird its blue upperparts. The bird then sought the heat of the sun, but misjudged things singeing his underparts, which turned orange, and his rump. When he got back, the flood had subsided and the ark was no more. Since then, the Kingfisher has been flying along rivers, searching and calling for Noah.

In *The Birds of Wiltshire*, by the Rev. A C Smith, which was published in 1887, we are told that, up until the early part of that century, it was not unusual for Kingfishers to be hung from the ceiling as an aid to weather forecasting. The theory was that the dead bird would turn so that where its bill pointed was where the wind was coming from, though in another story the bird becomes a compass and the bill points north.

In Greek mythology, Alcyone or Halcyone drowned herself in the sea to be with Ceyx, her husband, who had died when his ship went down courtesy of one of Zeus's thunderbolts. Instantly, the gods transformed Halcyone and Ceyx into Kingfishers (some versions of the story say that Ceyx became a Gannet or tern). Their fragile nest floated on the sea, and for a week either side of the winter solstice, the sea was calmed while the eggs were brooded. These were 'halcyon days', and until about 200 years ago, sailor superstition said that the seas were calm when Kingfishers were raising their offspring. Today 11 Kingfisher species are in the *Halcyon* genus and nine are in the *Ceyx* genus.

Detail from *Halcyone*, by Herbert James Draper (1863-1920). Kingfishers are flying over Halcyone's head.

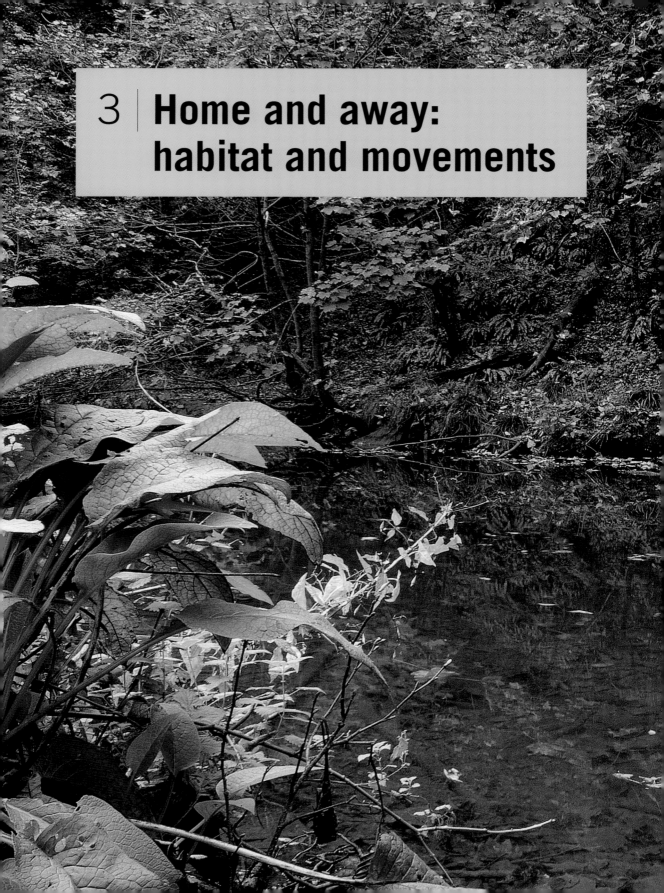

3 | Home and away: habitat and movements

When it comes to habitat selection, the Kingfisher it is not as fussy as you might think. The key requirements are water, plenty of fish, and, ideally, some perches to catch them from. These criteria apply all year round, with an additional breeding season requirement of somewhere to nest.

Still water or water with little flow is preferred, murky water is avoided, and in the breeding season at least, and for many birds all year round, this is a bird of freshwater habitats. It is a very capable catcher of fish but there are limits to the size of fish a bird of this size can tackle. A 10cm (4in) fish is about as much as the Kingfisher can manage. Good habitat has lots of fish that are smaller than this.

Ideal breeding habitat has a nest site near the water, typically a more or less vertical, or even overhanging, bank that is soft enough for tunnelling. It is not the norm, but if there is no alternative nest sites can be more than 250m away from where the birds feed.

Kingfishers can be found around rivers, canals, ditches, streams and lakes. They like some cover at the water's edge and perches to fish from, and prefer shallow water to deep water, presumably because it's easier to fish in shallow water. Despite their elusive character, they can sometimes be found very near human habitation. They will take short-cuts too, and may be seen flying across fields to save going all the way around a river bend.

This is not a bird of crashing, bubbling upland waterways, and does best in clean, unpolluted habitats. It is primarily a bird of the lowlands. Few live more than 650m (2,100ft) above sea level and finding one anywhere in Europe higher than 900m above sea level is very rare, though some have been found in Russia at around 2,000m (6,500ft) above sea level.

Wintering habitats

Some Kingfishers move to different areas for the winter. In the United Kingdom, most birds probably do not, though there are birds that migrate to the coast during this season and a few have crossed the sea to

This river is ideal Kingfisher habitat: clear water, perches and soft banks that are easy to tunnel into.

mainland Europe. Outside the breeding season, the species is more cosmopolitan in its choice of habitat and can be found in a wider range of watery environments. When not constrained by the need for a suitable nest site, some will forage in brackish water, and sometimes even in the sea. David Boag suggested that it was mainly immature birds taking fish from saline waters, and that these were probably birds that did not have a winter feeding territory.

Do they migrate?

Some Kingfishers migrate, and others stay put. When they do migrate, most do it under cover of darkness. Ornithologists believe that adults are less likely to seek sunnier climes than immatures, and if they do move they do not travel as far. Adult males are more sedentary than adult females.

Clearly, when your feeding area turns to ice, it makes sense to move on. Populations that breed in Poland, the Baltic States and Finland, and further east, across Russia as far as China and Sakhalin, are migratory and spend the winter in more agreeable climates in Europe, the Middle East and North Africa, with some from the far east of the global range travelling as far as the Philippines and Indonesia.

Most European migrants head south and west to spend the winter in less demanding parts of the breeding range. Some go further and do their

If you are lucky enough to live by a river, you may find Kingfishers right on your doorstep. This male has found a convenient perch at the edge of a riverside garden.

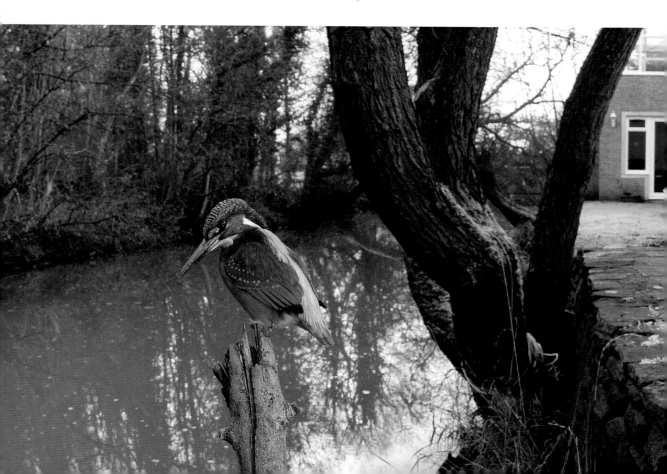

winter fishing in the Mediterranean or in North Africa, including areas where Kingfishers do not normally breed. Others make it to the Middle East and, even more remarkably, to India and Pakistan.

Birds in Central Europe are 'partial migrants': some migrate and some do not. Those that do move head for gentler weather to the south and west leaving those that stay to take the risk of falling victim to an unusually harsh winter.

Kingfishers that breed further west can be pretty sedentary though some around the Mediterranean head for the coast when summer heat dries out their favourite fishing patches. Those that breed in the UK do not migrate, although the few birds that manage to find somewhere to breed in the uplands may abandon their territories in winter. Data from bird ringing suggests that these birds travel no more than 25km (15.6 miles) from their breeding territory, and that individuals in the north of the country move a bit further than those in the south.

Germans call the Common Kingfisher the Eisvogel ('ice bird'), because of its southerly movements when waters freeze over. The Dutch name, Ijsvogel, means exactly the same thing. In the UK, severe winter weather can turn favourite fishing patches to ice and birds may have to go elsewhere to find food, frequently moving towards the coast. There is not much reliable data on this winter movement – ringing has thrown very little light on the phenomenon. When the birds do move, they run the risk of entering another Kingfisher's territory, where they will not be welcome.

How far do they travel?

The work of bird ringers gives us some clues about how far kingfishers travel, though only a small proportion of the birds that are ringed are found again – in the British ringing scheme, over three quarters of the birds that were found again were dead, the others were re-caught. A 1964 publication tells of two adults ringed in the former Czechoslovakia that took a southerly course to Italy, covering a maximum of 790km (495 miles). German birds have been recovered in Belgium, Denmark, France,

Spain and Italy. Some continental birds find their way across the sea from time to time, and pass through, or spend the winter in, the UK. Birds from France, the Netherlands and Germany have all been recorded in Britain. A youngster from Belgium was recovered in the UK and a bird showed up in Wales eight months after it was ringed in Brittany. Even more remarkable is a bird ringed in Wales that was re-caught in northern Spain less than three weeks later. Kingfishers ringed in Britain have also been found in France and Belgium.

The 'long-haul' experts seem to be the immatures. Adults do not tolerate their young for very long, and they are soon ousted from the breeding territory. A study in Russia showed youngsters moving up to 30km (19 miles) a day, and a young upstart from the former Czechoslovakia completed a marathon journey of 1,820km (1,140 miles) to south-east Spain. Other birds from the same part of Europe have made it to Malta and Sicily. The Russian study also found Kingfishers holding their first breeding territories no more than 20km (12.5 miles) from where they were born. In other areas distances of up to 128km (80 miles) are known. In Britain and Ireland, ringing data shows that birds moved an average of just 9km (5.6 miles) in the year after hatching and the adults seem even less adventurous – recoveries of dead adults average a mere 3km (1.9 miles) from the place they were ringed.

In surprising places

Kingfishers have been recorded from unexpected places. In March 1939, one showed up on the Skerries, a group of islands north-west of Anglesey. From time to time they are found on Scotland's Western or Northern Isles. These are places where they do not normally occur and records there may be of migrant birds from mainland Europe.

Sometimes the Kingfisher is seen in woodland, an unusual habitat for this species. My most unlikely sighting happened one June over 20 years ago when I was driving up a slip road onto the M11. A blue blur was flying to my left, more or less parallel to the road.

Opposite: Some north European Kingfishers migrate south and west to avoid cold winter weather, but not all of them do. A harsh winter can be serious if fishing patches freeze over.

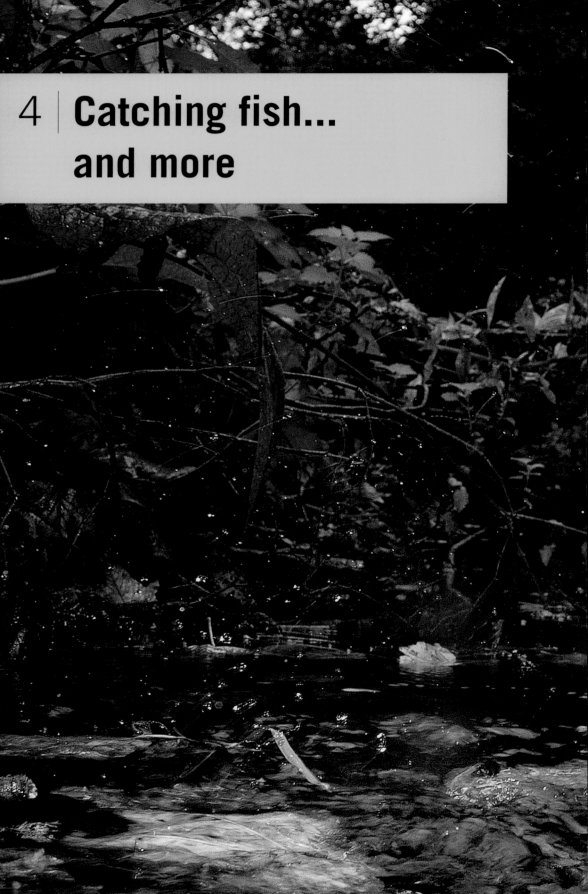

4 | Catching fish...
and more

The Kingfisher lives up to its name. Mostly, it eats fish, and the list of species consumed is impressive, including Bullhead (*Cottus gobio*), Minnow (*Phoxinus phoxinus*), Three-spined Stickleback (*Gasterosteus aculeatus*), loaches (*Cobitis* sp. and *Noemacheilus* sp.), Grayling (*Thymallus thymallus*), Carp (*Carassius* sp.), Perch (*Perca fluviatilis*), Pike (*Esox lucius*) and plenty more. As noted earlier, there is a size limit – a large Pike does not need to fear for its life when a kingfisher flies over. A small one might need to be careful though.

Kingfishers like their fish live, lean and not too long – up to seven or eight centimetres (2.8–3.1in) long is good, and even fish ten centimetres (4in) in length may be taken. David Boag attempted to work out how many fish a Kingfisher eats. To do this he put Minnows into an artificial pool, which they couldn't escape from, in a natural waterway. When he was reasonably confident that a bird was getting its sustenance almost entirely from that pool he could work out how many fish the bird was taking because he knew how many he was putting in. After 11 days of feeding, his conclusion, for a bird busy getting to know a potential mate, was that an average daily intake was 17.8 fish, which equates to about 46g (1.6oz) of Minnow-meat, just a bit more than the weight of the bird. The Kingfisher ate more fish when the sun shone, and less when it was cloudy.

Above and opposite: minnows and sticklebacks make ideal food for Kingfishers.

Another study collected data on the number of different types of fish eaten by Kingfishers in Belgium. About 36% of the diet was fish in the carp family (Cyprinidae). Three-spined Sticklebacks accounted for nearly 29%, with Bullheads being taken almost as often (about 28% of the diet). Other prey included Perch and trout (*Salmo* sp.). Further east, birds in Estonia are noted as particularly fond of Gudgeon (*Gobio gobio*), bleak

(*Alburnus* sp.) and Minnows. In the UK, work by Ron and Rosemary Eastman concluded that the birds they studied around the River Test in Hampshire devoured mostly Minnows, sticklebacks and Bullheads.

The Eastmans and David Boag tried to tempt Kingfishers to take non-fish prey items by providing alternatives where they could be very easily caught – the Eastmans put theirs in a tin bath in a stream. Their experiments were limited, but earthworms (Oligochaeta), Smooth Newts (*Triturus vulgaris*), crayfish (presumably *Austropotamobius pallipes*) and dragonfly larvae (Odonata) were all declined. When an elver was offered the bird had a go, but was unsuccessful and dropped it.

The seafood diet

Information on the gastronomic delights enjoyed by Kingfishers at the coast is harder to come by and earlier works have presumed that molluscs and crustaceans make up the bulk of the diet. They do take saltwater fish including goby (*Gobius* sp.), Tompot Blenny (*Blennius gattorugine*), Cornish Sucker (*Lepadogaster lepadogaster*) and Sand Smelt (*Atherina hepsetus*), and they are also known to eat prawns (*Palaemon serratus*).

Not fish again

Despite a predilection for things fishy, Kingfishers are sometimes more adventurous in their eating habits. From time to time, frogs are taken, much to the surprise of a certain Mr Topp, a taxidermist in Berkshire, who, according to a note in Volume 10 of *British Birds*, found a rather large one inside a dead Kingfisher – the frog's back leg was 6.4cm (2.5in) long! Kingfishers that live in the more arid parts of the Algarve take reptiles. Invertebrates aren't always safe either, and that includes the occasional land-based insect. Bugs, beetles, spiders, stoneflies, mayflies, shrimps and the larvae and adults of caddis flies and dragonflies have all ended up inside the Kingfisher. There are even records of Kingfishers going for bits of submerged plants, and during the very cold winter of 1859-60 one opportunistic individual in Norfolk, England, fed on suet that had been put on a bird table. There is also a record from Devon, England, of an individual that took suet, and was then fed from the bird table with bits of fish.

Skuas are infamous for their piratical stealing of food from other birds. Occasionally, Kingfishers play this game too and have been seen depriving the White-throated Dipper (*Cinclus cinclus*) of its hard-won catch. This despicable behaviour is not restricted to birds either – Water Shrews (*Neomys fodiens*) have also had their prey stolen.

Cough it up

It is not just owls that regurgitate pellets (undigested masses of food remains such as bones, fur and some insect parts). Other birds do too, including the Kingfisher. To find some, first find a Kingfisher's favourite perch – look for conspicuous white streaking from the bird's excrement. The area underneath the perch is a good place to look for pellets. Lots of the pellets land in the water but some land at the waterside. They disintegrate quickly, but a reasonably fresh pellet might still be more or less intact. Ian Llewellyn was able to watch the coughing up process. The bird gave up any attempts at fishing and sat fairly still for about 45 minutes before finally ejecting the pellet, which it shook out of the side of its beak. Once the pellet was out, the bird went fishing again. Ian also managed to retrieve a pellet very soon after it was regurgitated – a bird landed outside his hide, coughed up a pellet and flew off soon afterwards. The pellet was held together by a smooth coating and was covered in tiny bubbles, presumably giving the bird some protection from sharp bones.

Ian also found a pellet that he believed was produced by a bird that had struggled to find fish during a cold spell in January 2009. He had seen that the bird's hunting now included quick, short dives very near the river bank and suspected that insects and very small sticklebacks were being taken. Sure enough, when the pellet was examined, Ian found insect parts, which he believed were from a Water Boatman (*Notonecta glauca*) – these are illustrated above.

Pellets may be found close to Kingfisher perches. They usually consist of fish bones as seen in the two pictures on the left. The picture on the right shows insect parts from a pellet ejected during a cold winter spell. The insect remains, thought to be a Water-boatman (*Nononecta glauca*), suggest that fish were hard to come by.

A particularly dedicated ornithologist, or perhaps it was more than one, searched through over 14,000 bits of fish remains that had been deposited in pellets by some Belgian Kingfishers. Most of the remains (90 %) were from some sort of carp, or a Bullhead. This work was described in a paper by Hallet, published in 1977.

Catching ...

The Kingfisher is a dive-fisher par excellence. Experienced birds can enjoy a high success rate – Boag estimated that four out of five dives were successful, and with this hit-rate, the bird probably doesn't have to spend a large part of the day feeding. Work in Nepal, however, came up with a hit rate of just below 40%. It often dives from a perch, and Boag's observations led him to conclude that it prefers one that doesn't move much, and ideally, not at all. The Eastmans came to a similar conclusion. Normally, a fishing perch is one to three metres (3.25–9.75ft) above the water's surface, but some are higher. In 1976, R Frost and M Taylor watched a particularly intrepid bird that successfully fished the River Trent in England from an electricity cable roughly 11 metres (36ft) above the water. Ian Llewellyn has seen a successful dive into mini-rapids, with the bird popping up about 30cm (1ft) downstream.

The dive itself is remarkably speedy. Boag measured a bird's one metre (3.25ft) dive as taking about 1.2 seconds from perch to water to perch (with fish). When a Kingfisher needs a bit more momentum than a straightforward perch-dive provides, if targeting a deeper fish for example, it will fly up to begin the dive from a greater height. Powering wings add speed to the dive, the tail makes any final tweaks to its course, and the wings are pulled up over the bird just before impact. Mostly, the species is not a deep-diver, taking fish from just below the surface, to a depth of about 25cm (10in). Diving to about one metre (3.25ft) beneath the surface is not unknown however, and deeper fish need more vertical dives. Particularly shallow dives require a different technique. The head is retracted so that the bill barely protrudes beyond the chest and partly spread wings help to reduce the depth of the dive. Sometimes, the

Despite its dart-like appearance, the Kingfisher does not spear its prey. Occasionally fish become impaled on the bill, but if this happens the meal will usually go to waste because the Kingfisher cannot reposition the fish for swallowing.

Kingfisher forces hidden fish into open water by 'belly-flopping'. Dinner is served shortly afterwards.

When a diving Kingfisher enters its watery hunting ground, its eyes are closed but the bill is agape. Its underwater course has already been determined and no more adjustments are made. The bird's instinctive three-dimensional calculations of fish position, presumably informed by past successes and failures, are remarkable, and the Kingfisher can be unerringly accurate. The task now is to get back to the surface, a job made easier by beating wings and feather-trapped air, but with a final hurdle of breaking out of the water completely. Normally, an experienced bird leaves the water behind without problem, but rarely, a bird will struggle, only liberating itself after several considerable efforts.

This dive-fisher does not need a perch to dive from. In the absence of a solid launch pad, the Kingfisher hovers. It is not true hovering – if there is no breeze at all the bird cannot perform this trick. Hover-fishing is often employed around the coast and on estuaries. Hovering also enables the Kingfisher to snatch perched dragonflies from reedbeds (this has been observed in Spain) and they may even take sizeable spiders when they come out of their sand dune burrows. Hovering birds have also been seen doing Spotted Flycatcher (*Muscicapa striata*) impressions – with airborne insects as would-be prey, and a perched juvenile has been seen mimicking the insect-hawking attempts of other birds. Records of Kingfishers interrupting 'normal' flight, with an 'in-flight' dive win the blue blur even more respect as a king among fishers.

And despatching

Different prey items require different 'preparation' before they are swallowed. In essence, the despatch technique involves repositioning the fish so that it is gripped in the bird's bill a little forward of the tail, and quickly swinging it to the side to whack its head on something solid, typically a branch.

Sometimes the despatch is simple. A Minnow might need just one or two whacks before the squirming fish goes down the throat, or even none

Opposite: When there is no solid perch to launch from, the Kingfisher can dive from a hover. Unlike a 'true' hover, this kind of flight cannot be achieved without the help of a breeze.

at all. Fish with spines or spiny fins, sticklebacks for example, need more care for obvious reasons. Their demise must be well and truly complete before they are swallowed, or the spines still stick out. Inexperienced birds are sometimes too hasty, swallow too soon, and cough the uncomfortable meal up again before giving it a more thorough beating.

The Bullhead has substantial pectoral fins and it too requires extensive preparation before it is safe to eat. This fish is a choking hazard if the fins are sticking out. Beating does the trick. David Boag saw one determined bird whack a Bullhead 30 times. This wasn't enough. The fish went into the bird and back out again. Not once, but ten times. It took 57 more whacks to complete the job. The total preparation time was 13 minutes.

A vigorous head-shake by the successful hunter, shortly after the fish is swallowed, is the norm.

How did it do that?
In 1977 Philip Shooter was birdwatching with some friends in Derbyshire, England. They saw a Kingfisher dive from a perch about three metres (10ft) up. When it came up out of the water it had a fish.

What makes this unusual is that there was ice over the water, and snow on top of the ice. The bird had blasted through the snow and ice, latched onto a fish and came up out of the same hole it had gone in through. And it had done this even though some of the lake was not iced over. A favourite fishing patch and luck perhaps? While not quite as impressive, it is not unknown for a Kingfisher to choose an ice hole even when unfrozen water is available.

They do make mistakes

The Kingfisher is not a spear fisher – it grabs hold of its prey, it doesn't spike it. Not when things go well anyway. But occasionally, things go wrong and a fishing Kingfisher surfaces with a fish impaled on its beak, normally on the lower half. The bird kills the fish but the victim normally goes to waste, because the Kingfisher can't manoeuvre an impaled fish into the right position for swallowing. The fish is wrestled off the beak and dropped.

Sometimes a diving bird misses the target fish, and grabs something else instead, perhaps a stone. It can tell the difference though, and

Kingfishers hit their unfortunate prey against something solid, often a branch, before carefully manoeuvring it and swallowing head first. Spines and fins, as in the Bullhead above, are a choking hazard if they are not dealt with properly. Birds may cough up the fish more than once and beat it repeatedly before the meal is finally eaten.

normally drops the pseudo-fish pretty quickly. Fishing can also be too effective – the Kingfisher has been known to surface with two fish in its bill. When this happens the bird will whack both fish, get the innermost one into the right position for swallowing, and gulp it down. Unfortunately, while it does this, it loses the outermost fish.

Kingfishers can eat surprisingly large fish, but occasionally they are over-ambitious, and after a prolonged battle with their writhing prey, they will admit defeat and let the fish fall. It does not happen often, but sometimes so many fish have been eaten that a Kingfisher has to wait, perhaps for 20 minutes, gripping a fish in its bill, with the fish's head pointing away from the bird, until the bird is ready to swallow yet another fish – swivelling it round so that it goes down headfirst.

The winter of 1859–60 was a bitterly cold one in England. In Norfolk, a particularly hungry Kingfisher was creative in its hunting and took something that it really should have avoided. Gulping its meal down

To flatten its spines this stickleback must be thoroughly despatched before it is swallowed.

proved to be a fatal mistake. This desperate bird had tried to eat a shrew. The account by Rosemary Eastman does not specify which species of shrew the bird had tried to eat. Perhaps it was a Water Shrew (*Neomys fodiens*). This large shrew has poison in its saliva.

Special-eyes

The Kingfisher has elliptical lenses and excellent eyesight. Good quality optics are worth protecting, and the Kingfisher does this with its 'third eyelid', the nictitating membrane. Just before a plunge-diving bird hits the water, the nictitating membrane covers and protects the eye. When open, this membrane sits at the side of the eye, nearest the bill. When it closes, it crosses the eye horizontally.

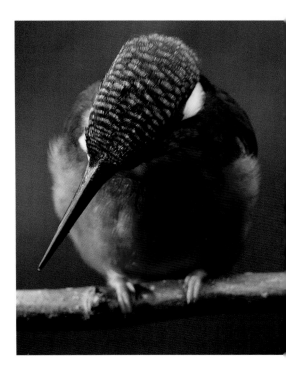

When it is fishing, the Kingfisher has to locate fish, select appropriate individuals for capture and consumption, and calculate their underwater position accurately. The fact that the prey is underwater makes the job even harder. Water plays tricks, but the Kingfisher can cope with them. It knows that the fish is deeper down than it looks – otherwise it would misjudge its dives and miss its target. Maybe it also knows that it won't be as big a meal as it looks either. Reflections from the water's surface, especially from a moving surface, can make things even more challenging. The bird keeps its eyes on potential prey, but as it can't move its eyes much, it does this with speedy head movements instead. A human eye has a single fovea, an area on the retina where the image is especially sharp. The Kingfisher has two foveae per eye. Some other birds do too, including hummingbirds, swallows, terns and eagles. It has forward-facing binocular vision and monocular vision to the sides. In each eye one fovea is for the lateral, monocular view and one for the binocular view in front. Should an unfortunate fish appear in the sideways facing fovea, a small head movement places the fish firmly in the bird's binocular view, where distances can be accurately assessed. The rest is history.

The Kingfisher has excellent eyesight and can fish successfully despite the reflections and distortions that its watery environment presents.

Feather care

Feathers make a bird a bird and they need to be very well looked after.
Those of the Kingfisher have to cope with frequent immersion. If a bird is
eating 17 fish a day, and has an 80% success rate on its dives, it will put
itself through over 20 dives in one day alone. Presumably, digging a nest
tunnel takes its toll on the plumage too, and
going in and out of one, especially a little later
in the season, certainly does. Feather
replacement through moult is vital and this has
been discussed elsewhere. Ongoing maintenance
is important too. Preening probably takes up a
substantial part of the Kingfisher's day – two
hours a day has been suggested. A single session
could fill 20 minutes if the job is done properly
and could involve bathing a few times as well as
the actual preening. During the preen itself the
bird uses its bill to apply oil from its preen gland
(which is on the bird's rump) to its feathers, to
'zip-up' any barbs that have come apart and to
make sure any wayward feathers are sitting
where they should. The Kingfisher works on
most of its plumage with its bill, but there are
some bits that are just too tricky to get at – it

uses a foot to scratch those hard-to-reach feathers on the head and the
back of the neck and will also use the lower surface of a wing to take care
of the top of the head. Some wing-stretching completes the routine.

Preening is a vital part of the
Kingfisher's day. Most of the
body can be reached with the
bill but birds will also use
their feet for hard-to-reach
places.

Adult Kingfishers are able to emerge from a dive without looking at all
waterlogged. An inexperienced youngster may not have mastered this
however, and the consequences may be terminal. If a young bird struggles
to remove itself from the water it will be a little sodden when it finally
extricates itself. Ideally, the immature bird needs to get its plumage back
into shape before another dive, but it may not do this and the sodden
youngster may drown or become too cold to survive.

5 | Finding and keeping a territory

How territorial is the Kingfisher? In a word – very. Don't be fooled by its gorgeous colours – the Kingfisher is a feisty creature, and many defend breeding and winter feeding territories. Most birds spend more than half of the year living a solitary existence. Breeding takes two of course, but as the breeding season comes to a close, male and female go their separate ways. Birds that winter around the coast seem to be less territorial, and are more tolerant of their fellow Kingfishers.

By early autumn, winter feeding territories are being secured. An adult male's winter domain is usually the same patch as his summer breeding territory. Ian Llewellyn watched a male in Avon, south-west England, that held a territory continuously for at least three breeding seasons and two winters. The female may hold a winter territory that abuts that of the male she bred with, or at least, is not too far away. Sometimes, the breeding territory is split between the male and female to form two winter feeding territories. These may overlap to some extent, but this is quite rare. David Boag watched a male and female that had bred together go on to share an artificially stocked fishing pool (effectively a bird table for Kingfishers) through a winter. They shared the easy pickings, but wouldn't fish there at the same time, even though they had previously fished in close proximity.

The Kingfisher's aggression is not only directed at other Kingfishers. An important perch in a bird's territory will not be shared lightly and the blue blur may chase impostors off – Boag saw the ousting of both a Grey Wagtail (*Motacilla cinerea*) and a European Robin (*Erithacus rubecula*).

Juveniles begin their lives in the territory that they hatched in, but their parents do not tolerate their presence there for long. For a while, they get along just fine with their fellow offspring, but there comes a point when the desire to 'own property' kicks in, and sibling relationships deteriorate.

Kingfishers are very territorial and may defend their patch with considerable aggression. If threat postures fail to intimidate, the birds will launch into battle, using bills as weapons.

This is a tricky time for the newly independent bird, and juvenile territory hunters turn up in surprising places, including garden ponds. At first, the youngster avoids advertising its presence. Kingfishers often give away their presence by their call, but the juveniles are smart enough to stay silent when they are new to an area. If they are on another bird's patch, and they are found, the territory owner will chase them off. But if no existing 'property owner' shows up, with time the incomer gets more vocal, though a little tentatively at first. Within a couple of days, the young bird could be shouting out its presence and ownership with full gusto calls as it flies around its new home. Birds that fail to secure their own winter feeding territory may be among those that move to coastal waters for the winter.

How big is a territory?

Ian Llewellyn's observations in Avon, England, suggest that there can be two or three nests on a 1.6km (1 mile) stretch of river. This is an average of one nest every 500m or so. Pairs tend to keep their distance from each other. On an Estonian river, the gap between pairs ranged from 300m to 1km, with as many as 15 pairs over 18km, while gaps of just 125m, and 150m have been recorded in Sweden and Scotland respectively. David Boag stated that there were plenty of territories that occupied as much as 3km or even 5km and a Belgian male had a home range that was nearly 14km long. With territories of this size, some parts are seldom visited, but unwelcome visitors, if discovered, will not be welcomed. Rosemary Eastman's work found that a pair would each have their own fishing patch in the breeding territory, but would not be above poaching a fish from their partner's stock. Clearly, territory size varies, but when one pair is just too close to another, stress levels are high and productivity suffers. The areas defended in the winter tend to be smaller than those defended in the summer, and during particularly cold weather more birds than normal may feed where food is in good supply.

A study in Estonia by Kumari, published back in 1939, concluded that a territory includes a core area that is particularly important to the male, and when birds gather food for their offspring, they fish in a feeding territory that is apart from the breeding territory, though usually within a kilometre of the nest. How this relates to other wisdom on Kingfisher territories is unclear.

What happens when rivals meet?

A Kingfisher will defend its patch with considerable zeal, be it a breeding territory or a winter-feeding territory. In-flight calls, and calls prior to landing, are the bird's declaration of ownership, but these don't keep out all unwelcome visitors and it is not unusual for impostors to show up. In a breeding territory both adults play a part in challenging other Kingfishers that dare to enter their patch, and will take them on either alone, or as a double act.

If an impostor is discovered, there's a roughly 50:50 chance that evicting it will need nothing more than a determined chase. But it is not always that easy. If the impostor is made of tougher stuff, things escalate, with the resident and the impostor beginning threat displays. When this happens, the gap between the two rivals is often about a metre (3.25ft). They stand tall with their feathers flattened and their shoulders up. Their wings sometimes sag forward and their eyes are firmly on their opponent. The bill is agape, a little elevated or pointing forwards on an elongated neck, and swinging unhurriedly from side to side, but not pointing at the 'enemy'. In the silence, the tension is palpable, but it dissipates if the display moves into aerial pursuit.

What then?

The 'upright threat display' can be a prelude to a 'forward threat display', where one or both birds gradually bends forward until it is nearer horizontal than vertical, perhaps lying, again with elongated neck, and sometimes swinging slowly from side to side. There could be jerky movements and calls, or no vocal accompaniment at all. By presenting a sideways view, threat displays may be a show of strength, enabling participants to show off the size of their bill. Opponents have been seen

Opposite: The straight back, beady stare and open bill show that this male Kingfisher is ready for a challenge. An upright threat posture such as this may be followed by more dramatic behaviour.

doing synchronized place swaps, and shifting slowly from one threat type to another, and back again. The threat repertoire also includes a stooped, spread-winged posture, and bobbing the tail.

If threat displays fail to oust an intruder, things can get very nasty and very noisy. A stream of varied, harsh, rasping calls breaks any silence that remained and the attacker takes to the air, intent on forcing its enemy off its perch. Bills are used as weapons. The birds may tumble down, and a watery wrestling match might ensue, each trying to get the other's head under water, perhaps even trying to drown the enemy.

Typically, battles do not last long, but there are records of fights carrying on for many hours. Ian Llewellyn has seen males posturing to each other outside a nest, with stretched necks and pointing beaks, for three hours. Neither bird conceded and the birds then fought physically, beak to beak and beak to wing. Ian has observed that when fights occur, they are often at nest banks or a territorial boundary. In 2009 he observed ongoing conflict between four birds near a nest hole in Bristol, England.

The low threat posture, seen to full effect in this juvenile, follows the upright threat posture. If neither opponent backs down, such aggressive posturing may lead to fights, especially when birds meet at territorial boundaries.

The encounter involved breeding birds that were determined rivals and a completed nest site – a recipe for war. The birds refused to back down and tensions built over three or four days, with huge aerial chases, high-pitched, staccato calls, stabbing attacks, attempts to knock each other off perches and plenty of exaggerated posturing. Sometimes, the males would take time out from the fracas and retire to their nest tunnel, leaving the females to battle it out. When these encounters are at their most intense, the combatants are so absorbed in conflict that they rarely fish and by the end of the day, they are panting and very tired. When neither male admitted defeat the battle ended with the females fighting in the water, with locked beaks, for five or six seconds. After that things calmed down.

David Boag suggested that the males get involved in more disputes than the females but Ian Llewellyn has seen more females fighting and is very clear that 'the most intense, sustained, aggressive and absolute' are the females.

There are also stories of aggressive encounters between two Kingfishers which are observed by a third, non-participating bird.

In the early part of the breeding season tempers can be very friable. Things can get particularly intense if pairs attempt to nest near their neighbours. In these situations a rival's hopes are sometimes foiled by a visit to their nest tunnel. This is not a social visit – the intruder is there to pierce the eggs. An account from Scotland tells of two nests that were close together with an unused tunnel separating them, that both pairs had rejected. A third pair adopted this nest, and laid seven eggs in it, but the eggs didn't survive long. The adults returned one day to find that their neighbours, who had young birds in their nests, had evicted the eggs.

Tired and confused?

To some people's ears, the call of the Dunnock (*Prunella modularis*) bears an uncanny resemblance to one of the Kingfisher's. It has even been known to fool a Kingfisher. David Boag recounts a tale of a Kingfisher, which had only just seen off an impostor, that heard a Dunnock call and went straight back into threat mode.

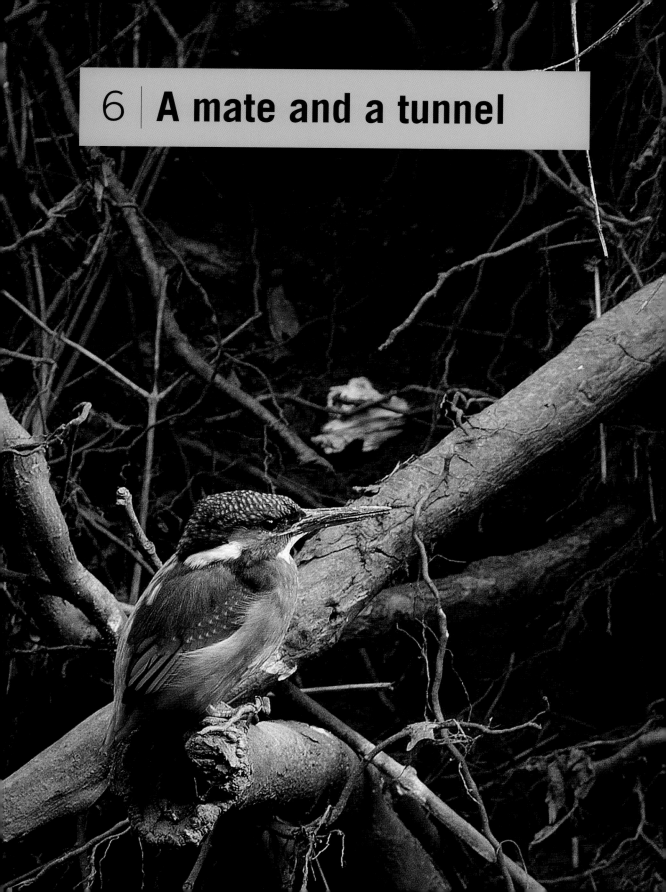

6 | A mate and a tunnel

After time spent alone the transition to life with a partner can be tricky. The Kingfishers that have survived the winter, including those that are less than one calendar year old, need to find a mate. By February, and sometimes earlier, Kingfishers in southern England can be looking for a partner. This may start a little later further north. After the relative quiet of the winter months, February and March can be one of the best times of the year to see and hear Kingfishers. The quest for a mate can begin quite sedately, with a perched bird declaring his presence with intermittent calls. A study by Heyn, published in 1963, describes a bird that kept this up for an hour before a potential mate made an appearance. The closer the new arrival got, the more bird number one called, until perches were abandoned in favour of an aerial chase.

Aerial wooing

Their high-octane courtship flights are noisy aerial pursuits that, in an instant, can take the two birds from just above the water to the tops of the trees, where they might settle, with high-pitched whistles drawing attention to their antics. Some energy-sapping chases last for hours and from an observer's point of view, it can be hard to work out if you are watching aggression or romance. The reality is that the chase could include elements of both. Normally, it is just two birds that take part in a courtship flight, but not always – five or more participants have been recorded. Courtship flights are at their most vigorous before the first brood of the season, but can be seen later in the year too, when they are performed, albeit with rather less zeal, as a prelude to the next brood.

More exotic courtship flights include approaching the female, perhaps more than once, with an elegant glide as the finale to a semi-circular flight that took the male out over dry land. Gliding is not a Kingfisher's normal flight mode. Both genders have also been seen flying gently on quivering wings, low over the water, and there is a record from *British Birds* in 1927 (contributed by W M Marsden) of non-stop 'singing' from two Kingfishers as they traced tentative circular flight paths 15–20 metres (c50–65ft) in diameter, with sporadic pauses in nearby bushes. A similarly vocal male was seen flying rings around a less energetic female, who remained perched (A van Beneden, 1930). The 'song' of the birds in question was described as similar to that of a European Greenfinch (*Carduelis chloris*) or White-throated Dipper (*Cinclus cinclus*), but not all Kingfisher aficionados are convinced that it really was that complex, and suggest that it was probably a simple series of differing whistles.

Love or hate?

At the beginning of the breeding season, a male Kingfisher can be quite uncomfortable in the company of a female and might, at first, display aggressively towards her. With time, things change. Both genders take part in the courtship display, but the males do it more, and they ham it up more as well.

The courtship display is not dissimilar to the 'upright threat' display. A displaying bird adopts a very vertical posture with its head pointing a little above horizontal and its wings draped forward so that the wingtips are as low as the hopeful performer's feet. Once again, the Kingfisher positions itself in a way that makes the size of its bill obvious. And if this were not enough to impress a potential partner, there is sometimes some soft whistling by way of vocal accompaniment. Courting birds take it in turns to whistle, and do not make this sound at any other time. As things progress, the gap between whistles reduces, so that ultimately, the illusion of a single note is created. Within a few days of pairing up, presumably as the pair bond becomes more secure, courtship displays become less frequent.

A male adopting a threat posture during courtship. This is not unusual early in the breeding season, when males are not at ease in the presence of a female.

A gift of fish

It may not work in our society, but it does the job for the Kingfisher. When the tentative ambiguity of early courtship is over, the male

Kingfisher presents his partner with the gift of a fish, and for a while this could take place a few times every day. The gift is sometimes a sequel to an aerial chase – after which the male leaves the female perched and goes fishing. When a male catches a fish intended for his partner, he swivels it round so that its head points out, contrary to the normal procedure when the fish is for his own consumption and the head must point in for safe swallowing. As he returns, there are animated contact calls from both parties – the male can call without letting go of his fishy gift. The female might now move closer to the male or do a bit of courtship displaying while he stoops, with wings lowered, and reaches towards her with his fishy offering.

The female quivers her wings as she takes his gift and the male might complete the ritual with a bit of courtship display. As an alternative, and to quote Ian Llewellyn, the male, with bill pointing to the sky, 'goes bolt

Once early courtship is complete, male Kingfishers will present their partner with fish, perhaps several times a day.

upright, fans his tail feathers and loops and dives like an Olympic diver, or loops and goes back onto the perch'.

David Boag describes the male, laden with a fishy gift, calling in flight (again, without dropping the fish) and using the female's response to pinpoint her position. Once perched, a subsequent, very short flight from either party, and a bit of sidling along the perch brings the pair even closer. Sometimes hungry females will beg for food from their partner and, in contrast to the grand fish-passing event described above, there are occasions when a female simply grabs the fish and gulps it down.

Is monogamy the only way?

For the Kingfisher, no it is not. Mostly, this species is monogamous, but not necessarily with the same partner from one year to the next. Where pairs are constant from year to year, and this is not unusual, it is likely to be two birds that carved up their breeding territory into two winter territories, with one territory for each bird.

It is also not unusual for a bird to change its mate from one year to the next, if, for example, an incomer has taken over their previous mate's winter territory.

Polygamy is not the norm, but it is far from unheard of, with a typical polygamous relationship connecting two females to one male. Different studies have produced different figures for the incidence of polygamy, ranging from 6% in a Swedish study by Svensson that looked at 116 'nesting associations' to about 35% on the Oka reserve in Russia (Numerov and Kotyukov 1979). Occasionally, the polygamy involves three females, and in one of the Russian examples above, because the females were double brooded, the male had his work cut out helping at six nests. Two females is more normal. The male may initiate proceedings with a second partner when the first is busy looking after eggs or brooding chicks. He might even abandon his first partner, leaving her with all of the hard work of raising the offspring. Sometimes both partners are at the same stage and the male incubates at one or both of the nests, leaving the remainder to the female.

Ian Llewellyn saw polygamy in action when a male mated with a second female just before his chicks with the first female fledged. He continued to take food to the first nest, but when his first partner ventured near the nest site of the second partner she was attacked by both the female, and the male, with the females fighting throughout the day.

Digging a hole for yourself

The Kingfisher's nest is a chamber at the end of a tunnel, and, soon after securing a partner, the search for an appropriate location is a priority. A pair either uses an existing tunnel or digs a new one, and after an energetic aerial chase, courting birds take a look at 'used homes' or begin to create one of their own. A 'used home' may be considered, and even worked on, before being rejected in favour of 'new build'. At this stage the male normally does the work. Boag's study found that most nest sites are being excavated in March, though work can take place in February and April too. Birds that take longer to find a partner do not have to contend with the vagaries of the weather to the same degree that earlier paired birds do. They court less before building, which starts sooner in the relationship, and seem to put more effort into excavating. As a consequence, late paired birds will normally be on eggs no more than a few weeks later than their more precocious neighbours.

Some birds go on to a second brood, and a few add a third. Often these are in the 'original' chamber, but sometimes a new nest is created. This can be nearby or quite a distance away – one was five-and-a-half kilometres from the original nest site, and this was for a brood that started before the first one had fledged.

An ideal nest site is easy to excavate and safe from predators and flooding. Nest tunnels are found in vertical, steep or overhanging banks on the edges of streams, rivers, canals, ditches and lakes, with no preference for banks facing in any particular direction.

Soft, sandy soils with no roots or stones make digging straightforward and being off the ground in a bank makes access trickier for predators, especially if there are no plants around the nest hole. On the other hand,

Opposite: The flash of a blue tail is the giveaway that this hole in the bank is the entrance to a Kingfisher's tunnel.

plants can help to hide the nest from animals one step up the food chain. Typically, the tunnel entrance is 90–180cm (3–6ft) up the bank, which affords a certain amount of protection from rising waters. There is an old record of a nest that was 36 metres (120ft) above the water's surface – presumably there was no danger of that nest flooding! Most tunnels are 50cm (1.6ft) or less below the top of the bank. Occasionally, Kingfishers will excavate a tunnel that is not by water, but this is unusual.

Some sites are used year after year, even when there are good alternatives in the area. Over a four-year period, Ian Llewellyn watched a poor quality Kingfisher bank that the birds persisted in using despite the fact that the nests were consistently either flooded or predated.

The ideal nest site has soft sandy soil that is easy to excavate. Male and female Kingfishers share the work of making the tunnel by pecking repeatedly at the bank until a foothold has been created and then taking turns to dig.

Other nest sites

Not all Kingfisher nests are in a 'standard' waterside bank. Some use the soil around the roots of a toppled tree. This could be more or less vertical and near the water but if they hit a root they have a problem and may well give up. Others use banks that are well away from the water – David Boag's book described a pair that bred in an earthbank in a patch of woodland. Other sub-prime sites include banks on minor country roads, nooks and crannies in caves, bridges, walls and the banks of railway cuttings.

Kingfishers are reported to very occasionally take advantage of another animal's labours, moving in to tunnels excavated by a Bank Vole (*Clethrionomys glareolus*), Sand Martin (*Riparia riparia*), or more surprisingly, a Rabbit (*Oryctolagus cuniculus*). And sometimes our own species gives a helping hand, deliberately creating artificial nest sites to encourage Kingfishers to breed. If the location and design are good the birds can be quick to move in.

Design and dimensions

The tunnel leading to the nesting chamber is usually around 45–90cm (1.5– 3ft) long, and either has a gentle incline towards the chamber or is horizontal. An incline aids the drainage of bird poo, which is an important function. Some tunnels are shorter and some are longer, depending, at least in part, on what the birds have had to dig through – a tunnel of just 15cm (6in) and another of about 135cm (4.5ft) have been recorded. The best tunnels are straight ones, as these are the most effective at allowing daylight into the chamber.

Ian Llewellyn's observations showed that Kingfishers are very picky about the diameter of the nest tunnel, digging a route in that is more or less 5.5cm (2.2in) across. This agrees with Zoller's 1975 study, though David Boag's work suggested that tunnels are created with a diameter of 6–7cm (2.4–2.8in).

The tunnel ends in a rounded chamber where the eggs are laid and the young looked after. The size of the chamber varies, but on average is about 11cm (4.3in) from top to bottom, and around 16 or 17cm

Once a foothold has been created the Kingfishers can start digging in earnest, using their bills to excavate a nest tunnel. The dimensions of the tunnel (as seen here looking out from the inside) are such that the birds cannot turn around until they have excavated or at least begun work on the chamber; instead they must walk backwards to exit, pushing loose soil behind them with their tails as they do so.

(6.3–6.7in) from left to right and front to back. The birds create a dip in the base of the chamber to increase the chances of their precious eggs staying put. They do not line the nest.

Excavating the nest tunnel is a shared task, with both male and female playing a part, though the male may do most of the work. The time taken depends, among other things, on how hard the soil is to dig and what obstacles are met on the way – stones or roots slow down progress and can force the project to be abandoned. When preparing the first nest of the season, the female might contribute almost as much as the male but if a second tunnel is excavated the male may do virtually everything. Most digging is done in the mornings and 7–12 days normally sees the job completed. Early paired birds can be a bit more leisurely, taking as long as two weeks to finish the project, while hard-working late paired Kingfishers can get the job done in as little as three days. If a second nest is excavated in the same season less time tends to be spent on it – usually 4–7 days.

Contrary to some established wisdom, Ian Llewellyn found that a male will sometimes check out existing tunnels and do a bit of digging alone, before he has found a partner. He also believes that birds investigate nest sites at any time of the year, though with increasing curiosity as spring approaches, and has seen a male with fresh mud on its bill in mid-November.

The technique

Excavation begins with the strange spectacle of a Kingfisher flying at a bank and pecking it. The male starts the process, flying from his perch without warning and pecking the chosen bank, with his partner nearby. He comes back to his perch and shakes or scrapes the soil off his bill, but may fly and peck repeatedly to secure the female's active involvement. When she does get involved both birds launch themselves towards their potential new home, pecking alternately at different spots on the bank. There comes a time when the apparent randomness disappears and all their efforts focus on one place. The aim is to create a foot-hold from which the Kingfisher does a passable impression of a woodpecker as excavation continues, one bird on, one bird off, each taking their turn. The 'excavator' can hear the muted whistles of its partner, who rests and acts as lookout. Should trouble appear the lookout's call changes and the construction site is quickly abandoned. Ian Llewellyn witnessed a digging operation that was abandoned for good because of the presence of a Eurasian Sparrowhawk (*Accipiter nisus*) in the area.

The muddy bill of this male suggests that he has been busy excavating. Kingfishers may investigate nest sites at any time of year but they are most focussed on nesting as spring approaches.

As the tunnel gets longer, things get easier unless, of course, they hit an obstacle. Digging birds use their feet to push the soil behind them as they progress. The dimensions of the lengthening tunnel are such that a tunnelling bird cannot turn around and has to walk backwards to extricate itself. As it does so, its tail turns the bird from excavator to mini-bulldozer and loose soil is pushed back down the tunnel.

Digging a tunnel is a bit of a hit and miss affair – hopefully, the chosen route will miss impenetrable obstacles, but sometimes of course, it

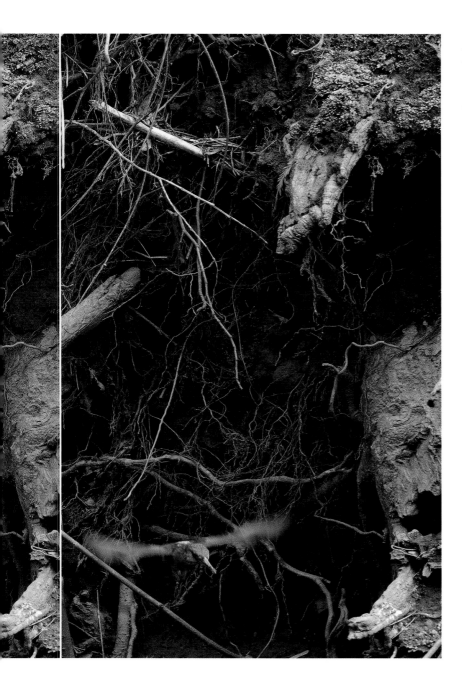

Male and female partners will take turns to excavate their nest. The site here is less than ideal for this pair; it has lots of roots to contend with and heavy mud.

hits them, and this could happen more than once before the birds choose a good spot. When it happens, one way forward is to dig around the object and try to remove it. If this is unsuccessful there are several options. The bird could complete the nest site with a bend in the tunnel, or, if it is deep enough in the bank, it could stop where it is and create the chamber by the barrier. Some birds elect to do neither of these, give up on the tunnel and start another one.

Finished

If you have the privilege of watching Kingfishers digging out their nest, there is an easy way of knowing when work on the chamber is at least underway. The narrow tunnel forces a tunnelling bird to come out backwards because there is no room to turn around. When the bird comes out beak first more space must have been created inside so work on the chamber must have begun.

Boag's observations indicated that mating normally takes place between mid-March and mid-April, when nest excavation is finished or nearly finished. Often the gift of a fish comes before the act itself, but not always. Ian Llewellyn has seen Kingfishers mating 9–12m (30–40 ft) up in a tree, though it usually takes place on a branch that is near the nest site and about 1.2–1.8m (4–6ft) high. The male's advances are not always welcomed, and an unwilling female makes her unco-operative state plain with her body language and a voice that has been described as both 'soft hissing' and 'angry'. A willing female may adopt a position similar to the head-up courtship posture described earlier. She quivers her sagging wings, and urges the male on with encouraging noises. He hovers. She virtually prostrates herself and the male seizes the moment. His feet are on her back and he holds her crown feathers with his bill. He can be quite rough, pulling the head around and flapping for balance. She gets her tail out of the way and his cloaca touches hers. The contact can be short lived – Ian Llewellyn estimates seven seconds or so – and genes for a future generation pass quickly from him to her. When the act is complete the male normally flies away, and perhaps bathes. David Boag saw the female fly off ten minutes later and Rosemary Eastman's account tells of a post-coital female that hung around for 15 minutes, at which point the male brought her a fish and she retired to the nest tunnel. Ian Llewellyn's observations include hearing the female utter a single chirp after mating.

Copulation starts with the birds alongside each other, and the male then hovering to get into position, or with the male perching above his mate and dropping down from there. Mating may be a less elaborate affair prior to a second nesting attempt, with much less preamble and no active encouragement from the female. Birds also mate less often second time round.

Mating usually takes place on a branch close to the nest site. Kingfishers do not usually mate until nest excavation is complete or almost complete.

7 | From egg to adult

In Greek mythology the Kingfisher's fragile, floating nest was said to have been made of fish bones. The truth is that Kingfishers do not build a nest of fish bones. They do not collect any material to deliberately line their nests but eating fish in a confined space means that with time, a layer of regurgitated fish bones and scales builds up, supplemented by the shed quill cases of the fledged youngsters. This is the 'nest'. Keeping the resulting 'fish bone cup' in one piece is very tricky, but apparently, there was a time when anyone who could find one and keep it intact would be very well rewarded, with the King of England offering a bag of gold and the British Museum £100 for one.

One nest chamber can see a pair of Kingfishers through the entire breeding season, even if they have more than one brood, though plenty of birds move to a different tunnel (or tunnels) after brood number one. Obviously, when broods overlap, a second tunnel is essential. If the pair goes as far as a third brood, it may return to its first nest.

Eggs and broods

A typical clutch consists of six or seven smooth, shiny, round, white eggs. Clutches as small as four are possible, and sometimes eight eggs are laid. One egg weighs just over 4g (0.1oz) and is about 23mm (just under 1in) long and 19mm wide. An egg is laid each day until the clutch is complete and incubation begins. In the Eastman's study they described the eggs initially as 'a delicate pink', which then turned white.

Kingfishers are usually single- or double-brooded, so, with clutches of 6–7 eggs, could produce 6–14 young in one season. Third broods are certainly not unknown. Boag found a three-brood pair that had lost their first brood to flooding and whose second and third broods overlapped. Domestic duties were shared, with the female taking care of the new eggs and the male ferrying food to the growing youngsters of their second brood. One male who kept two females was known to be triple-brooded twice over. That makes six broods, so if each of these had just six eggs in it, he would have sired 36 offspring that season.

Opposite: It is hard to believe that these newly hatched chicks will transform into one of our best-loved birds. A clutch of six or seven eggs is typical, and it is common for Kingfishers to have up to two broods in a season. Regurgitated fish bones and scales can be seen clearly in this picture.

Incubation

Both parents incubate and textbook wisdom is that the task is divided up more or less equally. Ian Llewellyn suspects that the females are a bit keener to incubate than the males and other studies agree with this. The Eastmans recorded males sitting for about three quarters of an hour, and the female for about an hour and a quarter. Zoller's 1980 study gives a sitting time of two and a half to four and a half hours.

Changeover can be a relatively simple affair. The absent parent flies towards the nest site, calling a few times, and settles nearby. The incubating bird comes out, and the other parent goes in. More elaborate changeovers also occur, with a bit of courtship display and food being

Both parents brood the young. Note the egg on the right of the chamber, which has become separated from the rest of the clutch and has been abandoned.

delivered to the previously tunnel-bound bird. Eggs are not normally left unattended though sometimes they are in the early stages when the birds are still working out the routine. The off-duty bird goes fishing, while the on-duty bird finds its way down the tunnel, moves to the back of the eggs and carefully manoeuvres into position. It uses its bill to move the eggs beneath its body, conveniently turning them in the process. Kingfishers do not seem to be the most observant or diligent of parents – an egg that has become separated from the others may be left to its own devices, with awful consequences. The sitting bird faces the tunnel entrance and might begin its stint with a relaxing preen. At some point, a pellet will probably be coughed up – the nest becomes increasingly unpleasant as things move on.

The Eastmans watched a second-brood nest and found that the female took responsibility for overnight incubation. The male presumably spends the night at a safe roost site, which could be a fair way from his eggs and partner.

Task allocation varies when a later brood overlaps an earlier one, which is not unusual. Males have been recorded incubating later clutches and leaving the female to look after the young of an earlier clutch. There is even a record of a hard-working male taking food to one set of offspring while doing a bit of incubation elsewhere. Both birds normally care for the last clutch of the year.

However the work is carved up, incubation takes about three weeks.

This vibrant female has just emerged from the nest after some time incubating.

Hatching

Because Kingfishers do not start incubating until all the eggs are laid, the young emerge at a similar time, with just a few hours between each hatching. The eggs have done their job and an adult will diligently take each broken eggshell out of the nest, airlifting it in its bill to take it away from the tunnel, and letting it fall into the water below. In some ways this is a strange thing to do, as the tunnel and chamber are certainly not a

model of hygienic living – with excrement, undigested fish bones and scales creating a 'special ambience'. Birds that build nests that are more accessible than the Kingfisher's make their nest and young less obvious to predators by removing the eggshells, but this is unlikely to be an issue for the Kingfisher. Scientists suggest that another reason to remove eggshells might be to make sure that the later hatching eggs in a clutch aren't impeded by empty eggshells.

The young Kingfishers are pink, blind, have no feathers and are totally dependent on their parents. They are brooded by one parent or the other for the first six to ten days and are fed their first fish dinner when they are just a few hours old.

Fish, fish and more fish

David Boag estimated that a typical nest of Kingfishers will, at its peak, get through more than 100 fish a day, and that is just the chicks. For the first week and a half or so, the adults bring relatively small fish in to feed the youngsters, limiting their catch to fish no more than 5cm (2in) long. As they make their way down the tunnel, they block out the light and, in response to the darkness, the chicks raise their heads. A chick gets a whole fish, and sometimes a surprisingly large one, taking it headfirst. Even at this stage, both mandibles are tipped with a flash of white, a distinctive feature retained on fledged juvenile birds. The white reflects what light there is, and may give the parent bird something to aim at. Getting the fish down is not always easy – David Boag saw a young Kingfisher wait for ten minutes with the tail end sticking out of its bill. Their guts must be very effective – in a matter of minutes digestive juices are breaking down the fish's head and making room for the rest of the meal.

The chicks are silent at first, but as their size increases so does the noise level. When they are about a week and a half old the youngsters get much noisier, making a continual churring noise that can be heard as far as 30m (100ft) away. It is probably made by just one bird at a

Opposite: By the time they are 12 days old chicks are very vocal and will call when they are hungry. The continual churring noise can be heard from 30 metres away.

Above: Chicks are fed whole fish by their parents. Initially, the adults choose smaller fish when catching a meal for their young. This male is about to enter the nest with a meal for one of his brood.

time – the one next in line for a fish, though Boag suggested that two birds may call at once. If the bird is not hungry the churring ceases, but soon starts up again when an adult comes back to the nest. The bigger the chicks get, the louder the noise becomes, but it stops if the birds sense danger.

By the time the chicks are a week old, the demand for fresh fish deliveries has risen. As a fish-laden adult flies home to an expectant brood, it might utter a *teee ti-tee ti-tee ti-tee* contact call and as it arrives at the nest the churring from within gets more animated. When the chick at the front of the brood has been fed it moves around to the back. In its eagerness to be fed, the young bird sometimes grabs hold of the adult's bill as well as the fish and a bit of a tussle takes place. But the chicks keep themselves in order, and the fed bird goes to the back of the crowd. When the next fish arrives the next chick is fed, and so it goes on, with the fish going down head-first of course. As much as 50 minutes can pass before a chick gets its next fish and if it dares to go for more than its fair share, its siblings will give it a good pecking.

Growing up

At seven days old, the chicks are more robust and much of the characteristic blue colouring is visible, albeit in muted tones, as feathers that have yet to emerge become visible through the skin. It may take five or six more days for the feathers to poke through the skin. When they do, they are encased in sheaths and bit-by-bit, the nestling is transformed into a mass of dull blue and orange spikes. As the sheaths break open the feathers appear, tip first, but this does not start until the birds are about three weeks old and is more or less finished a day or two before the birds fledge. The eyes begin to open at eight days old, or a little later.

As the chicks get older the parents are more likely to reverse out of the tunnel than to come out head-first, and when the chicks are two or three weeks old they organize themselves differently. They are more and more likely to line up side by side in rows, with their bills pointing towards the tunnel. By this age a hungry youngster will quiver its wings as it requests yet more food, and as the time to abandon their subterranean existence draws near, most of the dining takes place in the tunnel, rather than the chamber, and waiting in turn to eat tends to become a thing of the past.

Mostly, young Kingfishers eat fish, but not always. Ian Llewellyn watched a bird in Avon, England, bring Signal Crayfish (*Pacifastacus lenuisculus*) to the nest to feed the young. He saw ten visits and crayfish were the dish of the day on five of them. The crayfish were about the size of a man's thumb, with their big front claws missing, so presumably the bird had worked out how to de-claw them. At the time the river was brown with mud, which must have made fishing trickier than normal. Adults have been known to eat crayfish, but this may be the first time that crayfish have been recorded as food for nestlings.

Keeping it clean

The chamber reeks of regurgitated fish remains, from the youngsters and their parents, but the young birds aren't keen to sit in their own

These sixteen-day-old chicks have lined up in rows facing the tunnel entrance. Their feathers are encased in sheaths until the the birds are about three weeks old, giving the impression that they are covered in spikes.

excrement. They have seen the light, and to make life in the chamber more tolerable, they squirt their white stuff towards it, like a blast from a high-pressure hose. This helps to keep the chamber clean but turns the tunnel into a slimy, excreta-coated mess that the parents have to traverse many times a day, making frequent baths a necessity. And as the youngsters near fledging, their discarded feather sheaths are added to the previous weeks' leftovers. Once the young have fledged, the tunnel and chamber could be home to another brood, in which case the female might clear out the bones before taking matters any further.

Adults will continue to feed their young for a short while after they have fledged. This youngster begging for food will soon have to fend for itself.

Into the light

The nest is a quieter place just before fledging. Instead of calling the youngsters stretch their wings and preen their recently acquired feathers. There are limits though, and their vow of silence is conveniently forgotten if food is at hand when they give a rough *gred gred* call. The parents may be quiet too, and bring less and less food to their offspring. The departure itself can take place with no ceremony – a juvenile just flies out, and then another one, sometimes without a parent in attendance, as witnessed by the Eastmans. The parents are there sometimes, though, and studies by Heyn (1963) and Reinsch (1962) talk of the adults calling to urge the young on and out. Boag's work, however, saw nothing like this. Even if the bird is around it is not always the model of a good parent – the Eastmans watched a female that remained a detached observer and then left the area when one of her brood dropped into the water after just a few flaps, and was then rescued by Ron and Rosemary.

Generally, all the young leave the nest on one day, with gaps between departures of 10 to 20 minutes, though it can extend into a second day. There is no going back, and those that do not fall into the water head for a nearby perch or are taken fishing by one of their parents.

Kingfishers fledge after 23–27 days in the nest. Fledging rates vary – Clancey's 1935 study showed that 80% of the eggs that hatched made it to fledging; while Glutz and Bauer's 1980 publication gives a lower figure of 53.8% for Swiss Kingfishers, but that was based on the number of eggs that were laid rather than the number that hatched.

Independence Day

Juvenile Kingfishers move away from the nest site fairly swiftly. Within a day they can be 300 metres away and given a couple more days can be four kilometres away.

The adults will continue to feed the young when they are out of the nest, but not for long. To help its parent find it, a youngster gives a *chip* or *chip chip* call, a note that it has used since day 17 or 18 in the nest. This is probably the note that Ian Llewellyn describes as *chut*, but he is not aware of it being used in the nest. For a youngster to survive it must hone its fishing skills as soon as possible and will be diving on the same day that it fledges. Many flounder and become waterlogged; some drown, others make it to the bank only to perish there, while others dry out and live to dive another dive. Some do well – one was taking pond-skaters *Gerris* sp. just one hour after leaving the nest (Svensson, 1978).

Whatever the state of their fishing skills, the adults want the youngsters off their patch within four days of them leaving the nest and sometimes sooner. They will 'encourage' them to leave, by chasing and calling, if that is what it takes. David Boag saw an adult switch from feeding one of her offspring one minute, to driving another one out of the territory, and then telling the one she had been feeding to do likewise. Such oustings are accompanied by angry calls, making Kingfisher country pretty noisy when there are young to move on.

The evicted youngsters must look for their own territory, with no knowledge of who lives where. If they are fishing on another bird's patch that bird will want to move them on, but the incomer keeps quiet and if its presence goes unchallenged the new Kingfisher on the block will stake its claim.

8 | Life and death on the riverbank

According to data on the British Trust for Ornithology's website only just over 20% of the Kingfishers that fledge survive their first year – four out of five do not make it to their first birthday. This may sound grim but many bird species have similar mortality rates during this part of their life cycle. For the one in five that survive long enough to have a go at breeding, the odds improve, but not by much – every year, just over 70% perish and a typical life expectancy is just two years, though some live much longer. The British record is held by a Kingfisher that lived in Hampshire and made it to the grand old age of four and a half years. There are likely to be longer-lived British birds – a Belgian Kingfisher lived an astonishing 21 years and was still going strong.

Lethal weather

Particularly cold winters can have devastating effects on Kingfisher populations. When feeding areas freeze over, apart from any intrepid individuals who go in through the ice, hungry birds must avoid starvation by finding their food elsewhere, taking different prey or moving to a different area. In the freeze of 1889 dead Kingfishers were being 'picked up daily' around the River Kennet in the south of England. The winter of 1939–40 was so severe that the Thames iced over. Five years previously, a 68-mile (109-kilometre) stretch of the river was home to around 120 Kingfishers. After the freeze just a pair or two remained. In Britain, the icy winter of 1962–63 killed birds of many species. The blue blur had a very tough time – ornithologists think that 85-90% were lost. The cold of that winter was such that even estuaries iced over, so birds that moved to the coast would have struggled too. Cold winters in 1978–79 and 1981–82 also made an impact on the UK population, but numbers rose between the mid-1980s and in the years up to 2007. Severe winter weather in 2009–10 could have drastically reduced the population but, at the time of writing, its impact had not been quantified. A cool spell in the summer can make it harder to find food then too.

The hazards of the cold are not just the difficulties of finding food. One unfortunate Kingfisher settled on a metal pipe only to find that the frost 'glued' it to the metalwork. In its panic, the poor bird broke its leg in two places. It was rescued, but died later.

Floods also kill Kingfishers. Whole broods can be lost to breeding season floods and overflowing waterways make it much harder to find a meal.

Food for others

It is said that the Kingfisher's bright plumage consists of warning colours that tell any would-be predator that they taste awful. If this is true, it does not always work.

Many Kingfishers have perished during icy winters, and with climate change these conditions are likely to become more frequent. How Kingfishers will cope remains to be seen.

The Eurasian Sparrowhawk (*Accipiter nisus*) can grab prey in mid-air or take it from a perch, and it has certainly been known to take a Kingfisher. Ian Llewellyn watched a Kingfisher's response to a Sparrowhawk that had perched right above it. The Kingfisher went into a threat display, holding its vertical pose for about 15 minutes. Some predators are opportunists and one Kingfisher was in the wrong place at the wrong time when a Great Black-backed Gull (*Larus marinus*) flew over. The gull took the Kingfisher, flew off with it and perched, much to the disgust of John Gascoigne, the warden of a country park in southern England, and the birdwatchers that he was accompanying. John threw a lump of soil to encourage the gull to let go of its prey, but to no avail. The

Little remained of this female Kingfisher and her clutch of eggs after a Brown Rat had wreaked havoc in the nest chamber.

gull took to the air and gulped down its unusual meal.

Kingfishers are not totally safe from predators in the water either. 'My Halcyon River', a 'Natural World' film made by Charlie Hamilton James for the BBC showed two angry female Kingfishers fighting in the water. As if from nowhere, an American Mink (*Mustela vison*) appeared and took one of the birds. It tried to take the second bird too, but failed. In Sweden mink are known to predate Kingfishers at the nest and their feathers have been found in mink spraint.

It is not just mink that will raid a Kingfisher's nest. The Red Fox does it, and so does the Brown Rat. The Brown Rat could be a significant predator of Kingfishers. Ian Llewellyn has seen four nests, two in each of two successive years, on two rivers in Avon, England, all with full clutches of eggs, which were destroyed by rats. When one of the 'ratted' nests was investigated, the tunnel was clogged with soil, stones, moss, leaves and fish bones. Having eaten the eggs and the female Kingfisher the rat had left little behind and had made her own nest in place of the bird's. All that remained of the bird and the clutch was her bill, her left wing, some feathers, and some bits of eggshell. The rat must have gained access to the tunnel by holding on to a small root. Predation by rats was also recorded by Rosemary Eastman. This time the rat dug its way into the nest chamber and took a female and her chicks. All that was left over after this attack was the lower mandible, a bit of skull and some feathers. Every part of the chicks seemed to have been eaten. Ian Llewellyn suspects that Weasels (*Mustela nivalis*) take Kingfishers and Stoats (*Mustela erminea*) have also been listed as predators. One nesting attempt went badly wrong when a Common Mole (*Talpa europaea*) burrowed into the chamber, presumably accidentally.

Ian Llewellyn also observed some Kingfisher behaviour that he believes was an adult checking the tunnel for predators: he saw a female proceeding down the gloomy tunnel swinging her wide-open bill from side to side.

Domestic cats are often quoted as a significant predator of Kingfishers. Given the bird's lifestyle and the average cat's aversion to water it seems unlikely, but BTO ringing data suggest that it does play a part. Up to

1997, just over three quarters of the 737 ringed Kingfishers that had been found were dead. It was not always obvious what killed them, but a cause of death was given to 59% of the birds. Of these, 16% of deaths were attributed to 'domestic predators, mainly cats'. However, presumably some of those records at least are based on a cat showing up with a dead or dying bird. The cat may not have taken the bird – it may have picked it up after an unfortunate collision with a window or car.

Man-made hazards

Like some other birds, Kingfishers sometimes get it wrong and fly into windows, perhaps thinking that they have found a convenient short-cut. Others are killed by cars. BTO ringing data suggests that these are significant causes of death. Of the dead birds recovered where the cause of death is certain, 61% of the fatalities were attributed to humans, directly or indirectly. Most of these deaths were in road traffic accidents or the result of flying into windows. A different kind of human cause led to the death of a Kingfisher in 2010. The dead bird was found inside a factory in Kent, England. It had been ringed just over three years earlier and its routine flight path took it through the factory. The building was also its roosting site. An ailing economy meant that the factory, which had previously been working all week long, had to be closed for part of the week. The Kingfisher was trapped in the building and died.

Most anglers are responsible, but sadly, and probably slowly, a lost hook and line killed this Kingfisher.

Lost and discarded fishing tackle has been a threat to wildlife for many years. As the tragic picture above shows, victims include the Kingfisher. Ian Llewellyn took this photograph in Bristol, England, early in 2010.

Poison

The loftier your position in the food chain, the more likely you are to suffer from a simple ecological principle that sees toxins finding their way up the line and into your body tissues. This puts the Kingfisher at risk, with chemicals such as pesticides and heavy metals from farmland and factories finding their way into the waterways, and via their prey, in to the Kingfisher.

There are indirect consequences too. Pollution reduces fish populations making Kingfisher food harder to come by. And, as climate change brings periods of drought, and our demand for water rises, less water remains in our waterways, making the toxins even more concentrated.

A survival strategy

Given the day-to-day hazards that the Kingfisher must contend with, it is a good job that they are able to produce so many young, with decent clutch sizes and the capacity for a second or even a third brood. One would think that this would enable the species to make a relatively rapid comeback after a population setback, but this does not always happen. In the United Kingdom the BTO's Waterways Bird Survey, which ran from 1974–2007, showed a decline from 1974 that lasted about a decade. Then the population started to increase but didn't return to 1974 levels until about the year 2000. On a more positive note, Rosemary Eastman's monograph describes a quick recovery after the catastrophe of the 1939–40 winter, when the population on a 68-mile (109-kilometre) stretch of the Thames had almost recovered after just three years, and 1972's *London Bird Report* tells of a speedy comeback after the cold winter of 1962–63.

9 | Past imperfect; future tense?

Today the UK is home to an estimated 4,800-8,000 pairs of this glorious little bird. Its population goes up and down over time. It is currently on the amber list of Birds of Conservation Concern and the BTO has not identified any long-term population trend. But without a bit of 19th century bird protection legislation, things might have been very much worse. The bird's use as a weather forecasting tool (see page 37), which still took place in the early 1800s, was not good for the species, and neither was the 19th century boyhood urge to acquire one. Eastman's monograph talks of the possibility of the Kingfisher becoming extinct in England. That was written in 1969 and the author was wondering what might have happened without the 1880 Wild Birds Protection Act. The act came into being because of the efforts of the Victorian naturalists and 'sentimentalists' who campaigned against the persecution suffered by numerous bird species. It gave the Kingfisher a degree of protection in the close season (from 1 March until 1 August), though it remained 'fair game' during the open season. The 19th century had been a very tough time for the species…

Stuff it

Twenty years earlier, the bitter winter of 1859–60 had taken its toll of the Kingfisher population. Those that survived were not left to their own devices in the hope of a recovery. This was the Victorian era, and taxidermists were in demand. Stuffed birds were must-have accessories and that definitely included the Kingfisher, which became a victim of its own beauty. Taxidermists like to work with specimens that are in good shape, so to reduce 'damage' to their quarry, the bird catchers would work at nest sites and use a net or snare to take birds at the entrance. When they were taken the adults may well have had eggs or dependent young in the nest. The market for Kingfishers was very buoyant – one taxidermist is said to have acquired 100 dead Kingfishers in just a year. For the stuffers, dead Kingfishers were the stuff of dreams.

Previous page: An unusual view of the blue blur – Kingfishers diving at dusk.

Opposite: Another diving Kingfisher. Population sizes go up and down, but without Victorian bird protection legislation, their numbers could have plummeted even further.

Flaunt it

If you've got it, flaunt it, and Victorian ladies liked to flaunt bits of Kingfishers. Someone had to get those bits first of course – an 1864 account in *The Field* tells of someone shooting Kingfishers along the Thames for just this purpose. Once acquired, the specimens featured on hats and other items of 'finery', as feathers, a wing, or even the whole bird. Thankfully, tastes in fashion have changed.

Kill it

Its good looks made people want to shoot, it but it may have been the Kingfishers supposed incompatibility with the fishing world that caused it the most problems. The Victorian game fishing world believed that the species' appetite for salmon and trout fry was just too big to accommodate and Kingfishers were ruthlessly persecuted. Stones were pushed into nest tunnels so that access was impossible. Kingfishers were shot. Traps were set including the cruel pole-trap, which was outlawed in 1904. The pole-trap is a spring-trap tethered to the top of a pole. When a bird lands on it, the jaws spring shut around the bird's legs and the bird dies hanging upside-down from the pole. Perhaps the ultimate cruel irony was that Kingfisher feathers were used to make fishing flies. Trade in Kingfishers continued into the 1920s – nets intended for wildfowl took a by-catch of Kingfishers, and each dead bird meant an extra shilling in someone's pocket.

Poison it

The industrial revolution changed the way we live. Unfortunately, it also poisoned our waterways, which would not have been good news for the Kingfisher. It has been suggested that the Kingfisher population in 19th century Yorkshire may have suffered as a consequence.

On the up?

It seems that towards the end of the 19th century things were improving for Kingfishers in Britain. At the northern edge of its UK range, there were nests in mid-Scotland and in 1903 there was one in Stuartfield, just over 20 miles (32km) north of Aberdeen. A few gentle winters and the 1880 act were believed to have contributed to the bird's change of fortune. With much less persecution going on, life for the 20th century Kingfisher improved, and populations grew in some areas. But there were setbacks, including the killer winters of 1946–47 and 1962–63.

A healthy looking Kingfisher. The species' status in Scotland has improved since the 1960s, but the freezing winter of 2009-10 could have hit the population hard. At the time of writing, its impact had not been quantified.

In Scotland

BirdTrack is an online project of the BTO, the Royal Society for the Protection of Birds and BirdWatch Ireland. It brings together sightings from lots of birdwatchers to find out more about where birds occur and migration. Birdtrack records from 2008 show the Kingfisher in Scotland at a similar latitude to the 1903 record mentioned above, but this masks what happened during the intervening years. Those cold winters sliced through the Scottish population and polluted rivers are thought to have hindered any comeback in much of the country. By the 1960s the Scottish range had contracted with regular breeding reaching no further north than very southern parts of the country. Since then Kingfishers had been pushing north again, at least until the cold winter of 2009–10.

Elsewhere

Across the Irish Sea, the last quarter of the 19th century saw Kingfishers breeding throughout Ireland, but in many areas it was far from common. Information on 19th century persecution of the species in Ireland is scant, but 1954's *Birds of Ireland* suggests that it was a serious problem for the bird. Things improved through much of the 20th century but then took a turn for the worse.

In mainland Europe, to some degree at least, the story is a familiar one, and many populations have been hit hard by pollution and persecution. But it is not all bad news. The Belgian population crashed to 190 pairs in the early 1970s but recovered and was estimated as 900–1,500 pairs in the early years of this century. There is good news from the south of Poland where numbers seem to be increasing – in the 1960s, Kingfishers in this area were virtually consigned to history. The Austrian population has also done well after a very sticky patch from 1950 to 1970.

The current state of play

BirdLife International's verdict (2004) is that the European Kingfisher population was 'broadly stable' between 1990 and 2000. Its numbers were suspected to be declining in Spain, Slovakia, Turkey, Slovenia and Greece, and increasing the United Kingdom, Finland, the Netherlands, Denmark and Switzerland. At a European level, the population is described as 'depleted' because it has not fully recovered from a decline that finished around the early 1990s, and the Kingfisher is a 'Species of European

Common Kingfishers live in many parts of the world and, at a global level, are not a major cause for conservation concern. Long may it stay that way.

Conservation Concern'. Globally, the Kingfisher is doing okay.

In Britain and Ireland, the 1988–91 breeding atlas (a project co-ordinated by the BTO) records Kingfishers in most of England, much of Wales and some of Scotland with a good scattering of records across Ireland, particularly in the east and north-east. This work will be updated when the BTO's current atlas project is completed in 2011. Meanwhile, 2009's Birds of Conservation Concern puts the species on the amber list. The good news is that it is not one of the birds that the conservation world is most worried about. It is however, certainly one to keep an eye on.

To the future

Overall, things are not looking too bad for the Kingfisher. But there is no room for complacency and positive actions for Kingfishers will benefit other wildlife too. The Kingfisher is a great bird to watch, but make sure that you do not disturb it. Loitering near a nest site can be particularly dangerous as it can deter the parents from going in to feed the young. Eventually, things are compounded because the young will fall silent if they do not get enough food or become chilled. When this happens the adults are not getting any 'feed me' messages, so they stop bringing food to the chicks. In the UK, the Kingfisher is a Schedule One species, which means that it is on the 'most protected list' of 1981's Wildlife and Countryside Act. Aside from the ethical issues, disturbing the blue blur is an offence, which could see the offender in jail, facing a very hefty fine, or both.

If they are to thrive, Kingfishers need good quality habitat, with enough of the right fish and suitable nesting opportunities. Waterways need to be managed sensitively so that nest sites are not inadvertently destroyed by heavy machinery, and pollution needs to be kept under control so that the birds can enjoy some decent water. We need to use water wisely – drainage can damage Kingfisher habitat.

Climate change means that we are likely to experience more extreme weather, and that could include icy winter spells, floods and droughts, all of which can make life difficult for the Kingfisher. So do your bit to minimize the impacts of climate change.

10 | How to see a Kingfisher

This chapter gives you some practical advice that, hopefully, will help you to find and see Kingfishers. We have also included an appendix that lists some places around the UK that you can go to try to see this wonderful bird.

How to do it

- Find out where Kingfishers occur in your area – you may not have to travel very far. Check the local bird club's website – look for information about birdwatching sites or lists of recent bird sightings – either of these could point you in the right direction. Look in county bird reports to see where Kingfishers have been seen, or use a 'Where to Watch Birds' book to find a site with Kingfishers. Or just ask a local bird watcher. If that fails, get a map, look for some likely looking patches of water and go and explore.

- Think about timing. Kingfishers can be seen throughout the day and at any time of the year, though some sites only have them in the winter. Your chances

Scan possible perches for a view of the Kingfisher. Their blue plumage may betray their presence, but they are not always as conspicuous as this bird.

are better at some times than others however. I have seen Kingfishers very well early in the morning and they are especially obvious during February and March as the breeding season gets underway, and in the autumn when youngsters are being driven out of the parental territory. There are more around in the autumn too because of all the young birds that are out and about and these can be much more approachable than the adults.

- Learn their calls and use your ears. That is how you will discover most of the Kingfishers you see. You can buy recordings of bird songs and calls or listen to them for free online. Try the RSPB's website (www.rspb.org.uk/wildlife/birdguide) for example. Their calls will help you locate the bird – often the sighting will be of a blue blur flying low over the water.

- Check likely looking perches by the waterside, including distant ones. Scan the trees at the edge of a lake for example. The wider, shallower parts of a river may harbour more fish – check these carefully.

A clue for the Kingfisher detective! Patches of bright-white droppings can help you locate a bird's favourite perch.

- Look for Kingfisher poo patches on banks or trees. Fresh droppings are an oily-yellow colour but when they dry they become very white and conspicuous. The patches can be as big as a dustbin lid. With practice you might be able to find pellet spots too. Then sit and wait – unless it is the breeding season. If the perch is near the nest your presence could cause problems, so keep your distance. Remember that the Kingfisher is a Schedule One protected species.

- If you have found a safe place to sit and watch, try using a portable hide or make the most of natural cover. If the bird sees a bit of movement or picks out a human shape that could be the end of your Kingfisher encounter.

- Follow the Birdwatchers' Code. You can find it on the RSPB's website.

- Enjoy your time with this brilliant bird!

Kingfisher places

This list is a useful starting point if you want to see Kingfishers in the UK.

ENGLAND

Bedfordshire
- Priory Country Park, near Bedford (Bedford Borough Council).

Cambridgeshre
- Milton Country Park, Cambridge (Cambridge Sport Lakes Trust).
- Paxton Pits, near St Neots (Huntingdonshire District Council).

Dorset
Radipole Lake and/or Lodmoor, Weymouth (RSPB).

East Yorkshire
- Blacktoft Sands, near Goole (RSPB).
- Tophill Low, between Beverley and Driffield (Tophill Low Wildlife Group/Yorkshire Water).

Essex
- Fingringhoe Wick, five miles from Colchester (Essex Wildlife Trust).
- Lee Valley Country Park, two miles north of Waltham Abbey.

Gloucestershire
- Cotswold Water Park (Cotswold Water Park Society).
- Slimbridge (Wildfowl and Wetlands Trust).

Greater London
- Brent Reservoir, north London.

Greater Manchester
- Pennington Flash Country Park (Wigan Leisure and Culture Trust).

Hertfordshire
- Rye Meads, near Hoddesdon (Hertfordshire and Middlesex Wildlife Trust/RSPB).
- Tring Reservoirs (British Waterways/Friends of Tring Reservoirs/Hertfordshire and Middlesex Wildlife Trust/Thames Water).

Lincolnshire
- Whisby Nature Park, near Lincoln (Lincolnshire Wildlife Trust/local authorities).

Norfolk
- Cley, four miles north of Holt (Norfolk Wildlife Trust).
- Strumpshaw Fen, east of Norwich (RSPB).
- Titchwell, five miles east of Hunstanton (RSPB).

Northamptonshire
- Summer Leys Local Nature Reserve, near Wellingborough (Bedfordshire, Cambridgeshire, Northamptonshire and Peterborough Wildlife Trust).

North Yorkshire
- Fairburn Ings, (Leeds City Council/RSPB).
- Scalby Beck, north of Scarborough.
- Wheldrake Ings, eight miles from York (Yorkshire Wildlife Trust).

Nottinghamshire
- Colwick Country Park, near Nottingham (Nottingham City Council).

Oxfordshire
- Farmoor Reservoirs, near Oxford.

South Yorkshire
- Old Moor, near Barnsley (RSPB).
- Potteric Carr, near Doncaster (Yorkshire Wildlife Trust).

Suffolk
- Lackford Wildfowl Reserve, north-west of Bury St Edmunds (Suffolk Wildlife Trust).
- Minsmere, near Eastbridge (RSPB).

Warwickshire
- Brandon Marsh, near Coventry (Warwickshire Wildlife Trust).
- Kingsbury Water Park, Sutton Coldfield (Warwickshire County Council).

West Sussex
- Chichester Gravel Pits.

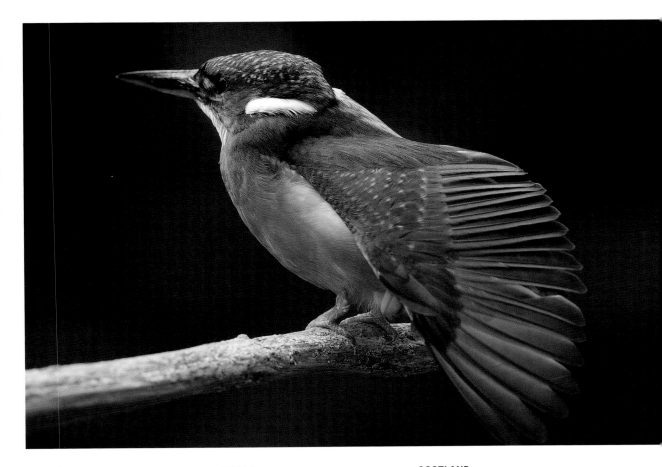

Wiltshire
- Cotswold Water Park (Cotswold Water Park Society).

Worcestershire
- Bittell Reservoirs, south of Birmingham.
- Upton Warren, near Bromsgrove (Worcestershire Wildlife Trust).

WALES

Caernarfon
- Conwy (RSPB).

Carmarthenshire
- Penclacwydd, south of Llanelli (Wildfowl and Wetlands Trust).

Pembrokeshire
- Welsh Wildlife Centre, south of Cardigan (Wildlife Trust of South and West Wales).

SCOTLAND

Clyde
- Barons Haugh, near Motherwell (RSPB).

Dumfries and Galloway
- Threave Wildfowl Refuge, near Castle Douglas.

Resources

Books

Boag, D., *The Kingfisher*, Blandford, 1982 and 1988.

Boag, D., *The Kingfisher*, Shire Natural History, 1986.

Brown, A. and P. Grice, *Birds in England*, T & A D Poyser, 2005.

Campbell, B. and E. Lack (eds.), *A Dictionary of Birds*, T & A D Poyser, 1985.

Cocker, M. and R. Mabey, *Birds Britannica*, Chatto & Windus, 2005.

Cramp, S. (chief editor), *Handbook of the Birds of Europe, the Middle-East and North Africa*. Vol. 4: *Terns to Woodpeckers*, Oxford University Press, 1985.

Eastman, R. *The Kingfisher*, Collins, 1969.

Elkins, N. *Weather and Bird Behaviour*, T & A D Poyser, 1983.

Flegg, J., *A Notebook of Birds, 1907-1980*, Macmillan, 1981.

Gill, F. B., *Ornithology*, second edition, Freeman, 1994

Harrap, S. and N. Redman, *Where to Watch Birds in Britain*, Christopher Helm, 2003.

Holloway, S. (compiler), *The Historical Atlas of Breeding Birds in Britain and Ireland: 1875-1900*, T & A D Poyser, 1996.

Lack, P. (compiler), *The Atlas of Wintering Birds in Britain and Ireland*, T & A D Poyser, 1986.

Mullarney, K. and L. Svensson, D. Zetterstrom and P. J. Grant, *Bird Guide*, HarperCollins, 2000.

Perrins, C. (ed.), *The New Encyclopedia of Birds*, Oxford University Press, 2003.

Sharrock, J. T. R. (compiler), *The Atlas of Breeding Birds in Britain and Ireland*, T & A D Poyser, 1976.

Wernham, C. and M. Toms, J. Marchant, J. Clark, G. Siriwardena and S. Baillie (eds.), *The Migration Atlas, Movements of the Birds of Britain and Ireland*, T & A D Poyser, 2002.

Websites

BirdLife International: www.birdlife.org

BTO: www.bto.org

Clements Checklist of Birds of the World: www.birds.cornell.edu/clementschecklist

IOC World Bird Names (version 2.1): www.worldbirdnames.org/index.html.

RSPB: www.rspb.org.uk

Surfbirds: www.surfbirds.com

DVD-ROMs

Birds of the Western Palearctic Interactive, Version 2.0, BirdGuides, 2006.

Other Titles by New Holland Publishers

Atlas of Rare Birds
Dominic Couzens. Amazing tales of 50 of the world's rarest birds, with stunning photos and maps. Endorsed by BirdLife. £24.99 ISBN 978 1 84773 535 5

Birds of Africa South of the Sahara
Ian Sinclair and Peter Ryan. Comprehensive field guide covering more than 2,000 species in full colour. £29.99 ISBN 978 1 86872 857 2

Chris Packham's Back Garden Nature Reserve
Chris Packham. A complete guide to the best ways to attract wildlife into your garden, and to encourage it to stay there. £12.99 ISBN 978 1 84773 698 7

Colouring Birds
Sally MacLarty. Ideal gift to help a child's developing interest in birds. Features 40 species outlines and a colour section. £2.99 ISBN 978 184773 526 3

Common Garden Bird Calls
Hannu Jännes and Owen Roberts. Useful illustrated book and CD featuring the songs and calls of 60 familiar species. £6.99 ISBN 978 1 84773 517 1

Creative Bird Photography
Bill Coster. Attractive and indispensable guide to all aspects of the subject, covering portraits, activities and 'mood' shots. £19.99 ISBN 978 1 84773 509 6

A Field Guide to the Birds of Borneo
Susan Myers. Features more than 630 species in colour. The only comprehensive and accurate field guide to the island.
£24.99 ISBN 978 184773 381 8

A Field Guide to the Birds of South-East Asia
Craig Robson. Acclaimed field guide covering 1,300 species, recently updated to include all the latest splits and discoveries.
£35.00 ISBN 978 184773 341 2

The History of Ornithology
Valerie Chansigaud. Beautifully illustrated account with many artworks and photographs and a timeline of events.
£17.99 ISBN 978 1 84773 433 4

The Naturalized Animals of Britain and Ireland
Christopher Lever. Fascinating guide to alien species, how they were introduced and their status, distribution and impact.
£35.00 ISBN 978 1 84773 454 9

New Holland Concise Bird Guide
Field guide to 250 species of British birds. Endorsed by The Wildlife Trusts. Also available: *New Holland Concise Butterfly and Moth Guide* and *New Holland Concise Wild Flower Guide*.
£4.99 ISBN 978 1 84773 601 7

New Holland European Bird Guide
Peter H Barthel. Pocket-sized comprehensive field guide to all of Britain and Europe's birds. Features more than 500 species.
£10.99 ISBN 978 1 84773 110 4

Tales of a Tabloid Twitcher
Stuart Winter. Remarkable ornithological news stories and gossip from the past two decades, as seen through the eyes of Fleet Street's number one birding journalist.
£7.99 ISBN 978 1 84773 693 2

**See www.newhollandpublishers.com
for further details and special offers**

Index

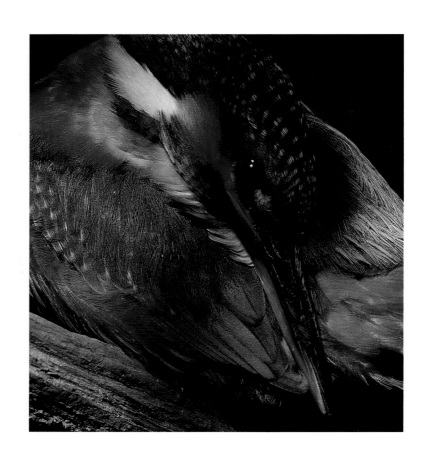